RICK PETERS

GREAT DECKS & PORCHES

A Step-by-Step Guide

STERLING PUBLISHING CO., INC.
NEW YORK

Acknowledgements

Butterick Media Production Staff

Photography: Christopher J. Vendetta
Design: Triad Design Group, Ltd.
Illustrations: Triad Design Group, Ltd.
Copy Editor: Barbara McIntosh Webb
Page Layout: David Joinnides

Indexer: Nan Badgett
Project Director: David Joinnides
President: Art Joinnides
Proofreader: Marci G Jaffer

Special thanks to Kris Jenkins at TimberTech, Marsha Sidmore with DIY Source, Inc., Rob Myers and Chris Mann at Screentight, Richard Wallace with the Southern Pine Council, Pam Allsbrook with the California Redwood Association, Brad Martin at Swan Secure Products, and the folks at Simspon Strong-Tie. Also, thanks to the production staff at Butterick Media for their continuing support. And finally, a heartfelt thanks to my constant inspiration, Cheryl, Lynne, Will, and Beth. **R. P.**

Every effort has been made to ensure that all the information in this book is accurate. However, due to differing conditions, tools, and individual skill, the publisher cannot be responsible for any injuries, losses, or other damages which may result from the use of information in this book.

Published by Sterling Publishing Company, Inc.
387 Park Avenue South, New York, N.Y. 10016
© 2001 Butterick Company, Inc., & Rick Peters
Distributed in Canada by Sterling Publishing
C/o Canadian Manda Group
One Atlantic Avenue, Suite 105, Toronto,
Ontario, Canada M6K 3E7
Distributed in Great Britain and Europe by
Cassell PLC, Wellington House,
125 Strand, London WC2R 0BB, England
Distributed in Australia by Capricorn Link
(Australia) Pty. Ltd.
P.O. Box 6651, Baulkham Hills, Business Centre,
NSW 2153, Australia

Printed in Hong Kong
All rights reserved

Sterling ISBN 0–8069–6643-2

Library of Congress Cataloging-in-Publication Data

10 9 8 7 6 5 4 3 2 1

Contents

Introduction

Adding a deck or porch to a home is one of the most common of all home improvement projects, and for good reason: A new deck or porch will increase your usable living space, provide you with a relaxing setting to enjoy the outdoors, and even create discrete areas for activities such as cooking, swimming, or play stations for the kids. What's more, adding one of these to your own home is a very doable project—as long as you're armed with the construction know-how—and that's what *Great Decks and Porches* is all about.

In this book, I'll start by taking you through the basics of deck and porch design. Chapter 1 launches into deck styles: freestanding, attached, single-level, raised, and multilevel are some of the more popular choices. To better understand these choices, you need to have a solid grasp of basic deck construction, including the two most important structural components: the ledger and the footings. Once you've decided on a basic style, there are numerous options to choose from, one of which is the pattern of the actual decking (such as diagonal, V-shaped, diamond, or herringbone). Next, I'll switch gears and take you through porch design and construction, including common terms and anatomy. Then I'll show you how to develop a plan to build a deck or porch, together with what you'll need to know about codes and obtaining permits.

Chapter 2 begins with an essential list of general-purpose and specialty tools you'll need to tackle a deck or porch job. Specialty tools include every-

thing from equipment for working with concrete and footings (such as power augers and water levels) to the gear you'll need to finish or refinish your deck (like power washers and garden sprayers). But the bulk of Chapter 2 is information that will help you wade through the many choices in materials, starting with decking options. Redwood, cedar, pressure-treated lumber, ipe, and the newest in composite boards (a mixture of wood chips and plastic) are all covered. There's information on hidden deck-fastening systems, the types of fasteners that work best for outdoor projects, framing connectors, and even ready-made parts such as balusters, railing, and post caps.

In Chapter 3, I'll go over the basic techniques you'll need to work on a deck or porch, starting with the all-important footings. Footings are so important because they transfer the load of the structure to the ground without allowing the deck or porch to sag or sink. I'll cover footing options; how to locate, dig, and pour footings; and how to install post anchors and the caps that allow you to connect the footings to the foundation posts. Fundamental to any construction project is making straight cuts in lumber. I've included a simple shop-made jig that makes this a snap. There's even advice on how to straighten the inevitable warped board and how to work with the new composite materials.

Chapter 4 takes you through the steps necessary to build a deck. Everything from site preparation to installing a ledger is covered (including how to install ledgers on sided, stucco, or masonry exteriors). There are detailed instructions on installing posts, beams, and joists to create a solid foundation for the deck boards. Both wood and composite deck board installation is covered in detail, as well as adding trim.

A deck, by itself, is a wonderful thing. But adding deck accessories, the topic of Chapter 5, will make it even better. The most common accessory for a deck is a railing system. I'll go over some of the options, including baluster and lattice variations. Then I'll show you how to install a railing system, starting with the posts and ending with a deck cap. Built-in benches are also a popular deck accessory, and there are step-by-step instructions on how to build three different types: post-supported, railing-supported, and a freestanding bench with no back. Finishing touches like skirting, fascia, and steps are also explained in detail.

Chapter 6 is all about overheads and porches. I'll start by going over design considerations and then move on to how to build a freestanding overhead screen. Next, I'll show you how easy it is to enclose an existing porch with a screen, using a nifty new product, along with how to add a screen door. Then there's detailed information on how to install a new porch foundation or new porch flooring.

In Chapter 7, I'll show you how to maintain and repair your deck or porch. I'll go over chemical options for cleaning and brightening as well as common finishes. There are instructions on how to clean and finish a deck and how to repair or replace deck boards, balusters, rail posts, stair treads, posts, skirting, flooring, porch columns, and even piers.

All in all, I hope that *Great Decks and Porches* will inspire you to tackle one of these popular and rewarding outdoor projects.

Rick Peters
Spring 2001

Chapter 1
Deck & Porch Design

Adding a deck or a porch to a house will enhance the value of the home while providing expanded living space and instant access to the outdoors. One of the toughest decisions you'll be faced with is what style deck or porch to add to your home. The variety of ideas and plans available is staggering. In this chapter, I'll help you wade through the choices, starting with a look at the various types of deck options available: freestanding and attached decks (*opposite page*), and single-level, raised, and multilevel decks (*see page 8*).

No matter which type deck you choose, you'll need to understand how one is constructed. On *page 9,* you'll find information on the two most common forms of deck support: ledgers and footings. You'll also need to know the lingo— *pages 10–11* provide an in-depth look at the parts of a deck and the terms used to describe them. On *pages 12–13* you'll find numerous deck board patterns to choose from.

Next, I'll take you through the parts and nomenclature of porches on *pages 14–15.* Here again, understanding construction and terminology will help you decide which porch style is best for you. Then, I'll show you how to develop a plan (*pages 16–17*). Finally, in case you're like me and enjoy

the math required to design a proper deck, I've included joist, decking, and beam spans on *pages 18 and 19.* On the other hand, if you're more interested in building instead of designing, consider purchasing plans; *see the sidebar below.*

DECK PLANS

Design it yourself or purchase plans? My answer? If you can find plans to fit your space, purchase them—let engineers and architects puzzle out all the details. A good set of plans will include the following:

- **Front, top, and side elevations**
- **Step-by-step directions**
- **Detailed materials list**
- **Accessory details such as planters, benches, stairways (if applicable), and railings**
- **Construction details (ledger connection, post and pier, and post-to-beam details)**

Check to make sure the deck has been professionally designed and meets or exceeds Uniform Building Code requirements. Though there are numerous deck plans available on the market, the plans from Somerset Publishing are some of the most complete and well-detailed plans I've come across. You can contact them at www.diy-source.com.

Deck Styles

Illustration courtesy of Somerset Publishing, © 2001

Freestanding

The simplest deck you can build is a freestanding deck (often referred to as a grade-level deck); *see the drawing at left*. Since this style deck does not attach to the house, it's really a wooden patio. This greatly simplifies construction, since the deck typically rests directly on concrete piers. As the ground freezes, thaws, and refreezes, the entire deck moves up and down as a unit—something that won't happen when one part of the deck is attached to the house (*see the section below*). Although you can find this style deck in a backyard, you'll most often find one in a remote location, such as near the edge of a lake or pond, or in a remote area of a property.

Illustration courtesy of Somerset Publishing, © 2001

Attached

Most homeowners want a deck that attaches to the home, as it provides access into the home and makes it easy to carry food and drinks back and forth for entertaining; *see the drawing at left*. One or more sides of the deck attach to the house via a structural member called a ledger (*see page 9*). The other end or ends of the deck are supported by a beam-and-post arrangement (*see page 10*). Since the end of the deck that's attached to the house remains in a fixed position, the other end must also remain fixed to prevent straining the foundation. That's why the footings that support the beams and posts must be below grade (*see page 9*). If they're not, the unattached end of the deck will rise and fall as the ground freezes and will eventually tear the deck apart.

Single-level

Single-level decks establish a transition between a house and a yard. For the smoothest possible transition, this style deck often does not incorporate a railing system into the design. Single-level decks are usually simple rectangles but can also feature curved or angled edges, like the deck shown in the drawing *at right.* These decks also work well as wraparound decks that follow the shape of the house. This style can then provide deck access from multiple rooms.

Raised Other than the single-level attached deck, the raised or elevated deck is the most commonly built deck; *see the drawing at right.* This style deck stands on posts anywhere from 1' to 10' or higher—basically whatever it takes to reach the main level of the home. One end of the raised deck attaches to the home via a ledger; the other end is supported by a post-and-beam structure. Because of this setup, raised decks are the solution to dealing with sloping ground and can also handle the varying floor plan of a split-level home.

Illustrations courtesy of Somerset Publishing

Multilevel Multilevel decks are by far the most complicated of all the deck styles, but they also afford the greatest design possibilities. Multilevel decks can handle steep slopes by breaking up the deck into different levels that step up or down the slope to hug it more closely. This style deck also lends itself to defining activity areas, such as a barbecue or pool area. Although a multilevel deck is basically two or more smaller decks joined together, the design of this style deck is best left to a professional, especially on those sites with steep slopes.

Deck Support

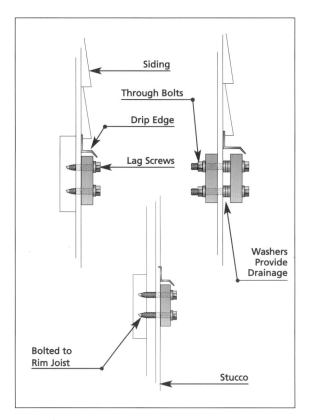

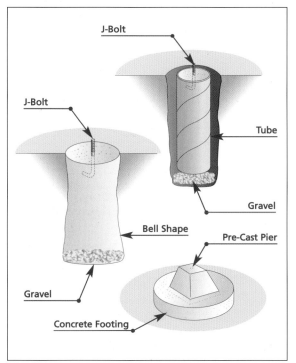

Unlike patios, which are installed directly on the ground, decks are built above ground for a couple of reasons. First, most homes require steps up for access, and raising a deck to the door threshold provides a seamless transition. Second, the foundations of decks are built of wood (usually pressure-treated). Although the wood is designed to stand up to the elements, it will last longer if kept clean and mostly dry. Raising it above ground accomplishes both. Deck support is provided by either ledgers or footings.

Ledgers
A ledger is basically a stout plank of lumber attached directly to the house to support one end of the deck; *see the drawing at left.* Its size depends on the weight of the deck and how it's attached to the house. How it attaches depends primarily on the home's exterior (siding, stucco, or brick). Common methods include securing it with lag screws and bolting it to the rim joist. Since a ledger must support one-half the deck weight, it's imperative that it be installed properly. Horror stories of decks shearing off the sides of homes and collapsing usually stem from an improper ledger installation. The best method is to bolt the ledger to the rim joist of the house *as shown.* To prevent moisture problems, install flashing above the ledger and insert washers between the ledger and the house to allow for drainage.

Footings
The other half of a deck's weight (or the full weight if it's freestanding) is borne by the footings. Footings are usually concrete columns set into the ground to distribute the load of the deck. The footing's diameter and depth depend on the deck's weight and the climate. For the average deck, an 8" to 10" diameter works well. In order for the footing to remain stable in all weather conditions, it must go well below the frost line (your local building inspector can tell you how far to dig). You can pour concrete directly into a hole or into a form; *see the drawing at left.* In temperate climates, precast piers can be installed on top of shallow concrete pads.

Deck Construction

Regardless of the type of deck you decide to build (or to have built, for that matter), it's important for you to have a basic understanding of deck construction, including the common parts and terms. No matter how simple or complex a deck is, every deck can be broken down into four main parts: the support system, the foundation, the decking, and accessories.

The support system

As I mentioned on *page 9,* a deck is supported by either ledgers or footings. A ledger attaches to the house to support one-half the deck weight, and concrete footings support the other half. The weight of the deck is transferred to the footings by way of posts and beams. In the drawing *on the opposite page,* the posts run vertically

between the concrete piers and a long, horizontal beam, which is often built up from 2-by stock. The beam can be located directly under the end of the foundation, or the foundation can extend past the beam to create a cantilevered deck, *as shown.* The beam can rest directly on top of the posts or can be bolted to the sides of them.

 # Common deck terms

Above-ground – a grade of treated lumber intended for use where the lumber will not come in contact with the ground.
Balusters – the vertical members of deck railing that divide up the space between the posts.
Beam – a structural member that transfers joist loads to the posts.
Blocking – 2-by material installed between joists to provide rigidity to the foundation.
Bracing – 2-by members designed to reduce the tendency of a deck to rack.
Cap rail –a railing member that is laid flat horizontally across the tops of posts.
Deck board – the floor board of a deck.

Fascia – nonstructural decorative trim installed around the perimiter of a deck to cover the joists.
Footing – a unit (usually concrete) used to support a post to transfer the deck load to the ground.
Frost line – the maximum depth at which freezing can occur; varies depending on location.
Ground-contact – a grade of treated lumber intended for high-decay hazards as when in contact with the ground.
Joist – a structural wood member that supports deck boards and spans the frame.
Lattice – wood strips formed into a grid used for screens and skirting.
Ledger – a structural member that attaches to the house and supports one end of the joists.

Overhang – the portion of a deck that extends beyond the posts or beams; often called a cantilever.
Post – a structural member that supports a beam and transfers the deck load to the footing.
Radius-edge decking (RED) – lumber produced for decking: 1" thick and 5½" wide with rounded edges.
Railing – a portion of a deck designed to enclose it; typically consists of a rail post, cap rail, and balusters.
Skirt – a screen installed below the deck to hide the foundation and limit access.
Stringer – the diagonal section of steps that supports risers and treads.
Tread – the horizontal portion of a stairway—the step.

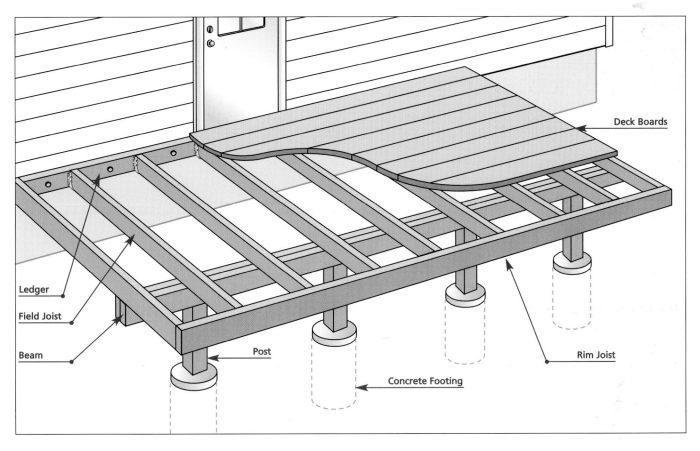

Deck Boards

Ledger

Field Joist

Beam

Post

Concrete Footing

Rim Joist

The foundation

In its simplest form, the foundation for a deck is an open frame similar to a framed wall that's lying on its side; *see the drawing above.* The structural member that attaches the frame to the home is the ledger. The joists that create the perimeter of the frame are called rim joists; these are commonly covered with decorative trim boards known as fascia. The joists inside the frame that connect the ledger to the opposite rim joist are referred to as field joists. The field joists typically attach to the ledger by way of joist hangers (*see page 30*) and are screwed directly to the rim joist or supported with joist hangers. To keep the field joists from shifting, they're either toenailed to the beam or attached with framing connectors called hurricane ties or seismic ties.

The decking

The most visible part of the deck, the decking (or deck boards) goes on last. In most cases, the boards run parallel to the house and attach directly to the foundation. Depending on the visual effect desired, you can install a wide variety of patterns such as diagonal, V-shaped, diamond, herringbone, angle-cut herringbone, and parquet; *see pages 13–14 for more on this.* Although deck boards made of wood—usually pressure-treated lumber, redwood, or cedar—are still the most common type, consider using one of the many composites available (*see page 26*). These new materials offer flat, stable decking that won't warp, and they require little or no maintenance over time.

Accessories

Most homeowners add a number of accessories to a plain deck, most often a railing around the perimeter, and steps leading off the deck in one or more locations. Other popular accessories are overheads to screen out the sun, built-in seating, and planters to showcase favorite flowers. (*For more on deck accessories, see Chapter 5.*)

Decking Patterns

Diagonal

There is a wide variety of decking patterns for you to choose from. It's important to note that the more complicated the pattern, the more work it will require—not only in laying the decking, but also in building the appropriate foundation. A diagonal pattern is one of the simplest variations, requiring only a modest amount of extra work, primarily in cutting the deck boards at an angle (*see the drawing at right*). This pattern can use the standard foundation that you'd build for a standard parallel decking.

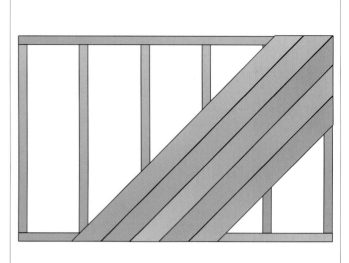

V-shaped

A V-shaped pattern like the one shown in the drawing *at right* is the next step up in visual interest. The only added step needed for the foundation is to add a double joist where the deck boards intersect. This extra joist provides added surface for nailing or screwing the deck boards in place. There's also slightly more work needed to cut the angles on the ends of the boards, as you'll have basically twice as many cuts as when installing a diagonal pattern.

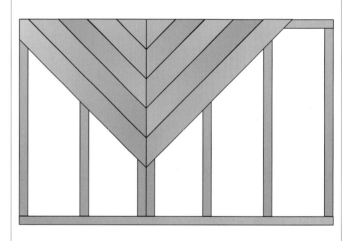

Diamond

Taking it up another notch, the diamond pattern offers nice visual interest while adding only two additional joists; *see the drawing at right.* These joists run parallel to the house and are centered between the ledger and the rim joist. Here again, they provide the necessary surfaces for attaching the decking. Just as with the V-shaped pattern, you'll need to spend more time making angled cuts because now you'll have four times as many as in the diagonal pattern shown *above.*

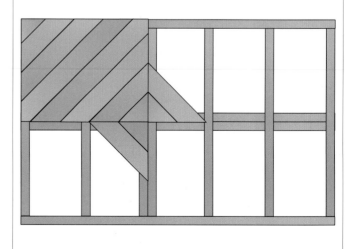

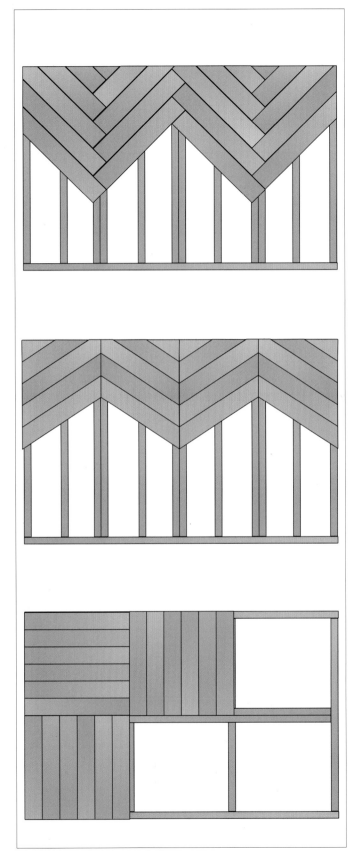

Herringbone

Of all the decking patterns, the interlocking deck boards of a herringbone pattern like those shown in the drawing *at left* offer one of the most pleasing deck patterns. But along with visual interest comes more work. This pattern requires double field joists wherever the pattern interlocks, to provide adequate fastening surfaces. Although fewer angled cuts are needed than in some of the other patterns, this pattern itself is complicated and requires lots of thought and advanced planning.

Angle-cut herringbone

Similar to the herringbone pattern, the angle-cut herringbone offers high visual interest and is slightly easier to install; *see the drawing at left.* As with the herringbone pattern, you'll need to double up the field joists wherever the deck boards intersect, for fastening purposes. All cuts are angled, and this pattern goes down surprisingly quickly once the starter boards are in place.

Parquet

The parquet pattern is a bit deceptive. It looks simple, but it requires a complex foundation to support the deck boards and provide adequate fastening surfaces. Not only do you need double joists wherever the pattern changes, but you also may need to add blocking inside the squares to support the deck boards—it all depends on the size of the "squares." If they're over 16" square, you'll need to add support. The advantage to this pleasing pattern is that the deck boards are all square cut and go down quickly once the foundation work is done.

Porch Construction

Porches are most often built as an entrance to a house and are usually roofed. With the exception of the roof, many of the construction details of a porch are similar to that of a deck. Differences, such as joist orientation and footings, are noted in the appropriate section *below*, along with a chart of common porch terms. All porches have five main parts: a support system, a foundation, flooring, accessories, and usually a roof; *see the drawing on the opposite page.*

The support system

Just like a deck, the support system of a porch starts with concrete footings set into the ground. The difference here is that instead of wood posts to support the foundation, most porches use brick piers for a better appearance. The brick piers are built directly on top of the concrete footings and often have skirting that spans between them to hide the foundation and limit access. The opposite end of the foundation attaches to the house via a ledger board to support the flooring. Since most porches are roofed, the footings must bear the weight of the roof as well and should be designed accordingly.

Common porch terms

Balusters – the vertical members of porch railing that divide up the space between the posts.

Beam – a structural member that transfers joist loads to the posts.

Column – a structural member designed to transfer the roof load to the porch foundation.

Fascia – nonstructural decorative trim installed around the perimeter of a porch to cover the joists.

Flooring – typically 1×4 tongue-and-groove boards installed across the joists perpendiclar to the house.

Footing – a unit (usually concrete) used to support a post to transfer the porch load to the ground.

Handrail – a member installed between columns or newel posts.

Joist – a structural wood member that supports flooring boards and spans the frame.

Knee rails – rails installed 3' above the perimeter of the porch; often used to support screening.

Lattice – wood strips formed into a grid that's used as screens, skirts, and overheads.

Ledger – a structural member that attaches to the house and supports one end of the joists.

Newel post – a member that supports a handrail where there is no column.

Pier – a brick or concrete unit that supports a column, header, or beam.

Post – a structural member that supports a beam and transfers the porch load to the footing.

Railing – a portion of a porch designed to enclose it; typically consists of a rail post, a cap rail, and balusters.

Riser – the vertical portion of a step or stairway, designed to support the treads.

Screening – metal or fiberglass mesh installed around the perimiter of a porch to keep out insects.

Skirting – a screen installed below the porch to hide the foundation and limit access.

Stringer – the diagonal section of a stairway that supports the risers and treads.

Tread – the horizontal portion of a stairway—the step.

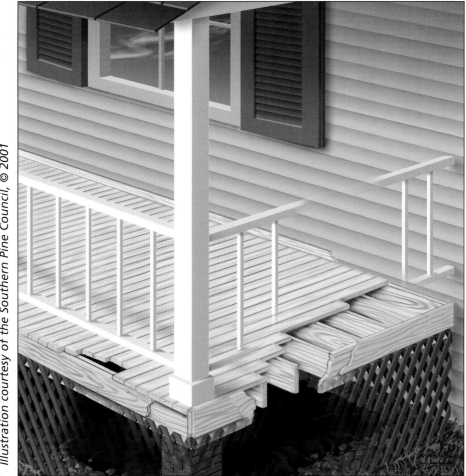

Illustration courtesy of the Southern Pine Council, © 2001

The foundation

The foundation of a porch is similar to that of a deck, with one big difference—the orientation of the field joists. Unlike the field joists for a deck, which are perpendicular to the house, the field joists of a porch run parallel to the house. This is because the flooring (*see below*) typically runs perpendicular to the house for better drainage. The joists connect to a double 2-by beam that rests on the piers. The foundation typically slopes ¼" per foot away from the house for optimum drainage.

The flooring

The standard in porch flooring is 1×4 pressure-treated tongue-and-groove flooring. It is installed perpendicular to the house to help the porch shed water. In most cases, the flooring is painted with a high-quality porch enamel.

Accessories

Common porch accessories include steps and a railing system that may or may not use the columns used to support the roof (if applicable). Since porches are such a highly visual part of a home, great care is usually taken in choosing and installing the railing system. Balusters are often turned or shaped into interesting profiles.

The roof

In most cases, a porch roof is an extension of the house roof. It is supported with columns of varying size and shape. For optimum support, the columns should rest directly over the brick piers and footings. The interior ceiling of the porch is most often covered with tongue-and-groove boards, and decorative trim and molding is applied to cover gaps and serve as transitions between the roof, ceiling, and walls.

Developing a Plan

As I mentioned on *page 6,* I heartily recommend buying a set of engineered deck plans. A good set of plans will provide, as a minimum, the following views: front view (*see below*), top view, and 3-D or architect's view (*opposite page*). Along with these you'll need numerous construction detail drawings, such as the ledger connection to the house, the post-and-beam detail, and drawings for steps and railings if applicable.

That's not to say that you can't design your own deck—many folks enjoy customizing one to fit their house. You just need to make sure to run the plans by your local building inspector (most inspectors require the same views provided by a good set of plans: front, top, and 3-D). For that matter, you'll need to run any ready-made plans by them, too, to make sure they meet or exceed local codes.

One of the first things you'll need to do before you buy a set of plans or design your own is to determine the amount of slope (if any) where the deck is to be installed. The easiest way to do this is to attach a mason's line to the house roughly at deck level and extend it out past the anticipated end of the deck. Attach a line level to the mason's line to make sure it is level, and then measure up from the ground to determine the slope; *see the photo at top right.* Check the slope at the midway point as well, and then make a rough side elevation drawing, noting the slope at various points. As you'll discover on *pages 37–38,* knowing the amount of slope is one of the key elements in designing a deck.

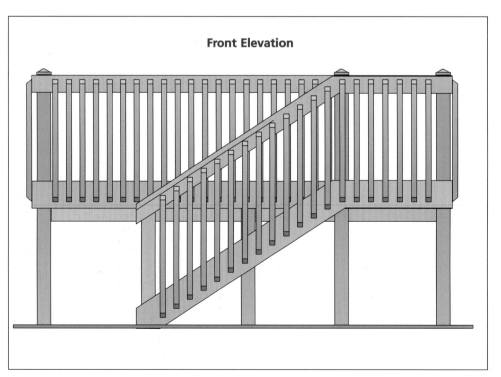

Front Elevation

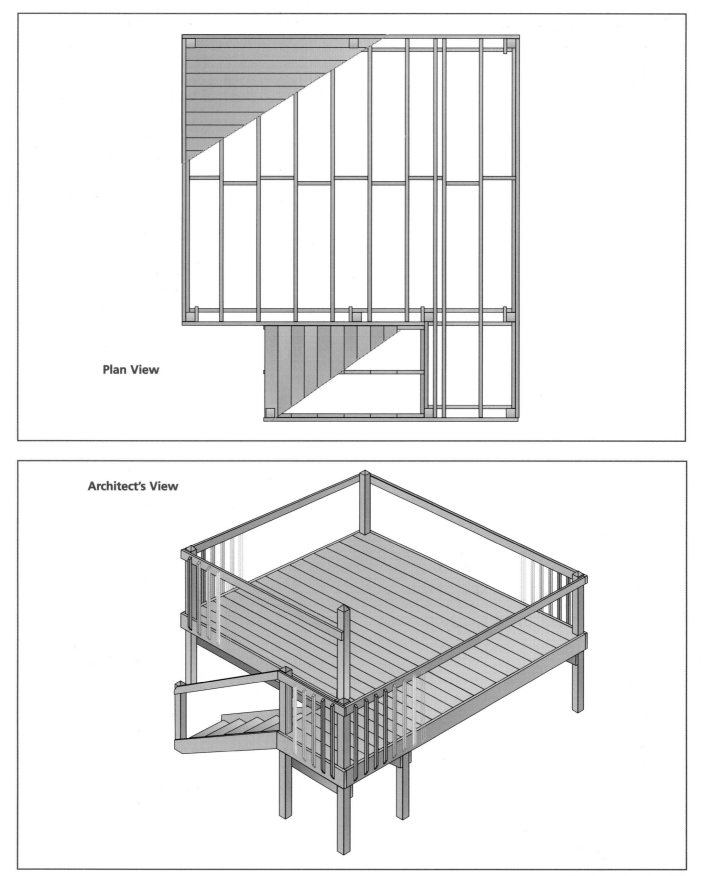

Plan View

Architect's View

Codes and Permits

Any deck or porch construction project requires approval from your local building inspector, including the issuance of a building permit. Once you've received the permit, make sure to check to determine when and how often they'll want to inspect the work. This can be once the footings have been dug, after the concrete is poured (before backfilling!), and after the foundation is installed, plus a final inspection after the deck or porch is complete.

If you want to design your own deck, start by choosing the type and size of deck boards, as this will determine the joist spacing (see the chart on the opposite page). Next determine the size of the joists—this is determined by finding the species and size of joist that can handle the spans required for your deck. For example (assuming 16" OC spacing), say the deck you're planning is 12' deep and 16' wide. You'll need joists that can span 12'. Checking the chart below, you'll discover that you could use a 2×8 in either Douglas fir–larch or hem-fir, or else a 2×10 in Douglas fir–South, spruce-pine-fir, or Western woods. Obviously, it's essential to know what wood you're buying.

Then you'll need to determine the size of beam required to support the joists (in the case of our example, 16'). Checking the lower chart on the opposite page, only one beam can span 16' of foundation unsupported: a single 4×10 of Douglas fir–larch or Southern pine. Note that the chart also supplies the maximum allowable distance between the posts that support the beam: 6'. By varying the number of footings, you can get by with shorter and smaller beams.

Maximum joist spans

Species	Joist Size	12" OC	16" OC	24" OC
Douglas Fir – Larch	2×6	10' 9"	9' 9"	8' 1"
	2×8	14' 2"	12' 7"	10' 3"
	2×10	17' 9"	15' 5"	12' 7"
	2×12	20' 7"	17' 10"	14' 7"
Douglas Fir – South	2×6	9' 9"	8' 10"	7' 9"
	2×8	12' 10"	11' 8"	10' 0"
	2×10	16' 5"	14' 11"	12' 2"
	2×12	19' 11"	17' 4"	14' 2"
Hem-Fir	2×6	10' 0"	9' 1"	7' 11"
	2×8	13' 2"	12' 0"	10' 2"
	2×10	16' 10"	15' 2"	12' 5"
	2×12	20' 4"	17' 7"	14' 4"
Spruce-Pine-Fir	2×6	9' 6"	8' 7"	7' 6"
	2×8	12' 6"	11' 4"	9' 6"
	2×10	15' 11"	14' 3"	11' 8"
	2×12	19' 1"	16' 6"	13' 6"
Western Woods	2×6	9' 2"	8' 4"	7' 0"
	2×8	12' 1"	10' 10"	8' 10"
	2×10	15' 4"	13' 3"	10' 10"
	2×12	17' 9"	15' 5"	12' 7"

Maximum decking spans

Species	Nominal Decking	Recommended Span
Douglas fir, Southern pine, Hem-fir, Spruce-fir-pine, Ponderosa pine, Redwood, Western cedar	Radius-edge decking (4" to 6" widths)	16"
Douglas fir, Southern pine, Hem-fir, Spruce-fir-pine, Ponderosa pine, Redwood, Western cedar	2×4	24"
Douglas fir, Southern pine, Hem-fir, Spruce-fir-pine, Ponderosa pine, Redwood, Western cedar	2×6	24"

Maximum beam spans

Species	4'	6'	8'	10'	12'	14'	16'
(2) 2×6							
Douglas Fir–larch, Southern pine	7'	–	–	–	–	–	–
Hem-fir, SPF, SPF–South	6'	–	–	–	–	–	–
Ponderosa pine, redwood, cedar	6'	–	–	–	–	–	–
(2) 2×8							
Douglas fir–larch, Southern pine	9'	7'	6'	–	–	–	–
Hem-fir, SPF, SPF–South	8'	6'	–	–	–	–	–
Ponderosa pine, redwood, cedar	8'	6'	–	–	–	–	–
(2) 2×10							
Douglas fir–larch, Southern pine	11'	9'	8'	7'	6'	6'	–
Hem-fir, SPF, SPF–South	10'	8'	7'	6'	–	–	–
Ponderosa pine, redwood, cedar	9'	8'	6'	6'	–	–	–
4×6							
Douglas fir–larch, Southern pine	7'	6'	–	–	–	–	–
Hem-fir, SPF, SPF–South	7'	6'	–	–	–	–	–
Ponderosa pine, redwood, cedar	7'	–	–	–	–	–	–
4×8							
Douglas fir–larch, Southern pine	10'	8'	7'	6'	–	–	–
Hem-fir, SPF, SPF–South	9'	7'	6'	–	–	–	–
Ponderosa pine, redwood, cedar	8'	7'	6'	–	–	–	–
4×10							
Douglas fir–larch, Southern pine	12'	10'	8'	7'	7'	6'	6'
Hem-fir, SPF, SPF–South	11'	9'	7'	6'	6'	–	–
Ponderosa pine, redwood, cedar	10'	8'	7'	6'	6'	–	–

Chapter 2
Tools & Materials

Building, repairing, or maintaining a deck or porch doesn't require a lot of sophisticated tools. It can, however, require a considerable amount of labor—particularly when you're building a new structure. Although you might think the tough part is cutting and nailing or screwing all the parts together, it's not. The real work comes from grunting around heavy wood slabs and beams.

A typical 12' pressure-treated 2×8 weighs over 100 pounds. Multiply this weight by the 20 or so joists that you have to install, and it can add up to a long day and a sore back. With this in mind, I always recommend having a helper to move timbers around. Even if you're young and strong (and not old and wary of your back, like some of us), a helper will make the entire job go a lot faster.

Materials choices, on the other hand, are numerous. With the advent of composite decking, the decision on what material to use for deck boards just got a lot tougher. That's because although composites cost more than the commonly used pressure-treated lumber, they are comparable in cost to many of the higher-end solid-wood choices available, such as cedar, redwood, and ipe. Also, many of the composites are virtually

maintenance-free—something that you'll really appreciate over the long haul.

In this chapter, I'll start by going over the general-purpose and specialty tools that you'll need for deck and porch work (*pages 21–23*). Then I'll jump into the many materials options you have to choose from—everything from redwood and cedar to the new plastic and wood composites (*pages 24–26*). Next, I'll describe just a few of the hidden deck-fastening systems available, which create a deck surface with no visible fasteners (*page 27*).

Regardless of the materials you choose, you'll need to know about the different fasteners for deck and porch construction and how to choose what's best for your project. I'll cover screws and nails (*pages 28–29*), framing connectors (*pages 30–31*), bolts and lag screws for heavy-duty fastening (*page 32*), and finally, the different ready-made parts you can purchase to help speed up the installation (*page 33*).

General-Purpose Tools

Demolition Many of the deck and porch jobs that you'll tackle will require some demolition work. You'll find the following tools useful for this type of work (*from left to right*): screwdrivers for general dismantling, a sledgehammer for persuading stubborn parts to come apart, a pry bar for pulling out boards and nails, a cold chisel or set of inexpensive chisels for chopping out holes in walls or flooring, a claw hammer for general removal, and a cat's paw for removing nails flush with or below the surface.

Measuring One of the most critical steps in any deck or porch installation is measuring and laying out the project, particularly the foundation. The tools *shown* should be in every homeowner's toolbox: a 25' tape measure; a framing square to check for perfect right angles; a folding rule for short, accurate measurements; a combination square to check for right angles; and a speed square to take quick, short measurements.

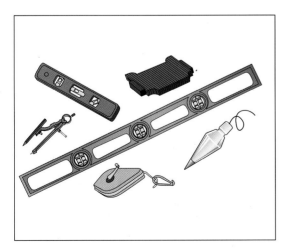

Layout In addition to measuring, laying out intended work is critical to the success of any deck or porch installation. The following tools should also be in your toolbox: a 4'-long level and a shorter torpedo level for checking framing members for level and plumb, a compass to draw circles and arcs, a contour gauge for laying out odd shapes, a plumb bob and string for transferring location points for footing and piers, and a chalk line for striking long layout lines.

Cutting tools Deck and porch work requires only a couple of specialized tools for cutting. Although you can cut dimension lumber and trim with a handsaw, it'll be a long day (or days, most likely). If you don't own a power miter saw, or "chop" saw, consider renting one or borrowing one from a friend. In addition to this, you'll need a wood chisel and a block plane for fine-tuning the fit of parts; a compass saw for cutting notches in framing members and flooring; and a pocket knife or utility knife to trim shims, etc.

Power tools Power tools can make quick work of many of the tedious tasks associated with building a deck or a porch. *Counterclockwise from top left:* a reciprocating saw for demolition work; an electric drill with a ½" chuck for large-diameter holes; a cordless drill with a ⅜" chuck for smaller holes; a right-angle drill for tight spots; a saber saw for cutting access holes; and a cordless trim saw for straight-square cuts.

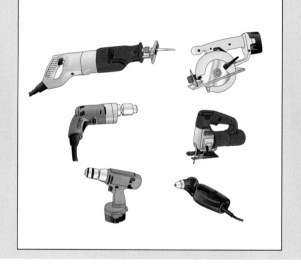

Safety gear As with any home improvement work, it's important to protect yourself by wearing appropriate protective gear. Keep the following on hand (*clockwise from bottom left*): leather gloves to protect your hands; safety goggles to protect your eyes; knee pads not only to cushion your knees but also to protect them; ear muffs or plugs for when working with power tools; and a dust mask or respirator to protect your lungs from sawdust (particularly the dust from pressure-treated lumber) and from the fine dust raised during demolition.

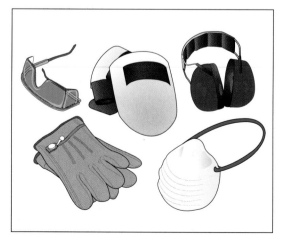

Specialty Tools

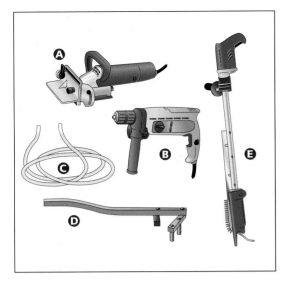

Deck tools Although not required, there are some specialty tools that can make a deck installation go a lot smoother. Shown here are a biscuit joiner (A) for installing hidden deck fasteners (*see page 27*), a hammer drill (B) and masonry bits for efficient drilling into concrete or other masonry, a water level (C) for leveling parts at a distance (such as the ledger and support posts), a deck board straightener (D) to encourage warped deck boards to behave, and an autofeed screwgun (E) that allows you to drive in deck screws without bending over.

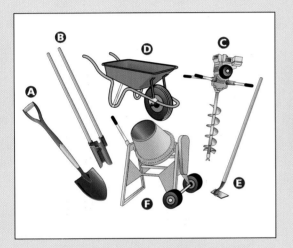

Concrete work If your deck or porch project calls for concrete work, you'll need some special tools. For digging post holes: a spade shovel (A) and a manual post-hole digger (B) (often referred to as a clamshell digger)—or better yet, rent a power auger (C) and save your back. For mixing and pouring concrete you'll need a wheelbarrow (D) and a garden hoe or mason's hoe (E) . If you've got a lot of concrete to mix, consider renting a portable cement mixer (F).

Cleaning and refinishing There are a few tools that are particularly useful for refinishing a deck or porch: a pressure washer, a garden sprayer, and a stiff-bristled broom. Pressure washers combine air power and water to make quick work of clearing dirt and debris off a deck or porch. If you don't want to invest in buying one, consider renting one for a day. A standard garden sprayer is the best way to apply deck cleaners, brighteners, and sealants. A stiff-bristled broom is often necessary to persuade stubborn dirt and stains to disappear. Smaller "disposable" deck brooms are available at most home centers.

Deck Board Materials

Redwood Redwood is both beautiful and durable (*see the photo at right*). Its decay resistance, insect resistance, and great longevity are legendary. The sapwood of California redwood is nearly white; the heartwood is light red to deep reddish brown. The grain is straight with a coarse texture. There are over 30 grades of redwood, varying in appearance and durability. For more information on which grade is best for your project, contact the California Redwood Association at www.calredwood.org.

Photo courtesy of the California Redwood Association, © 2001

Western red cedar Western red cedar (*see the photo at right*) is moderately soft and light in weight, is extremely decay-resistant, and exhibits little shrinkage. Completely nonresinous, this is one of the most decay-resistant species in America, hence its popularity in deck and porch construction. Cedar is also a dimensionally stable wood that lies flat and stays straight. Its tendency to split makes it perfect for shingles and shakes; when exposed, it weathers to an attractive silver gray. For more information on Western red cedar, contact the Western Red Cedar Lumber Association at www.wrcla.org.

Recommended deck board spans

Type of Deck Board	Pressure-Treated Pine	Redwood	Western Red Cedar	Trex	TimberTech	Ipe
Nominal size – maximum recommended span	Radius-edge decking – 16"	Radius-edge decking – 16"	Radius-edge decking – 16"	Radius-edge decking – 16"	Tongue-and-groove – 24"	1×4 – 28"
	2×4 – 24"	2×4 – 24"	2×4 – 24"	2×4 – 20"	2×6 – 24"	5/4 ×6 – 38"
	2×6 – 24"	2×6 – 24"	2×6 – 24"	2×6 – 20"		2×4 – 54"
				2×8 – 20"		

Southern pine Southern pine is the most common wood used in outdoor construction, as it's the least expensive (*see the photo at left*). It's usually treated with chromated copper arsenate (CCA), which imparts a greenish tint to the wood. There are two common "grades" of pressure-treated lumber: above-ground and ground-contact. Each describes how much preservative is retained by the wood: 0.25 pound per square foot in above-ground lumber, and 0.40 pound per square foot in ground-contact lumber, which can touch the soil or be buried in the ground. For more information on Southern pine, contact the Southern Pine Council at www.southernpine.com.

Ipe Tropical hardwoods are becoming an attractive, albeit expensive, decking option. Most of these hardwoods are very dense, naturally resistant to insects, and extremely durable even under the worst weather conditions. Ipe is a related group of South American hardwoods whose color ranges from rich russet to reddish brown; *see the photo at left.* Since it is a hardwood, ipe requires predrilling before fastening to prevent splitting. The natural color can be preserved with a water sealant; or ipe can be left untreated to age to a weathered gray. For more information on ipe, contact Timber Holdings Limited at www.ironwoods.com.

DECK "CAPS"

Here's a nifty alternative to tearing up and replacing worn-out deck boards. Anchor Decking Systems has developed Durable Deck, a vinyl deck "cap" that can be installed directly over an old and worn-out decking—even over concrete; *see the photo at right.* The only requirement is that the old surface be structurally sound. The deck cap is screwed directly to the old decking and then the screws are concealed with a snap-in vinyl strip. Durable Deck is available in six colors and 12', 16', and 20' lengths. For more information on Durable Deck, visit their Website at www.durabledeck.com.

Solid composite decking Although composite decking has been around for years, it's finally starting to show up in local lumberyards and home centers across the country. Manufacturers make composite deck boards from recycled plastic and ground-up wood fibers with the intent of offering the best of both materials. Because part of the composition is wood fibers, the decking will weather gray over time; since the wood fibers are small, there is no risk of splinters. The benefit of adding plastic is that the deck boards are much more stable—no warp—and they don't split. Trex, Choice-Dek, Tek-Dek, and Nexwood are all popular choices.

TIMBERTECH®

Of all the composite decking choices out there, my favorite is TimberTech. Unlike the solid composites described *above*, TimberTech is an extruded composite in the form of tongue-and-groove planking; *see the photo and drawing at right.* An extrusion like this is expensive (typically around $4 a square foot), but it offers a number of excellent advantages. First, as with any tongue-and-groove product, the fasteners are hidden—no nail "pops" or protruding screws to catch a bare foot. Second, with support "braces" engineered into the planks, the end result is a dimensionally stable and lightweight deck board that will stand up extremely well over time.

Although it's not required, TimberTech can be finished with a high-quality oil-based paint or solid color stain after it has weathered. If left untreated, it will weather to a natural driftwood gray (*as seen on the deck on the cover of this book*). End caps and fascia boards are available to cover the exposed ends of the planks. *See pages 65–66 for more on installing this type of decking; for additional information, visit www.timbertech. com.*

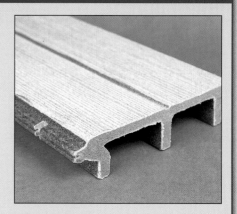

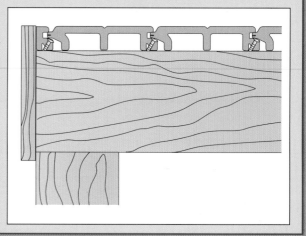

Hidden Deck-Fastening Systems

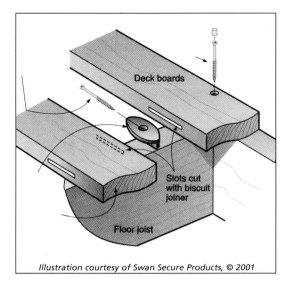

Illustration courtesy of Swan Secure Products, © 2001

EB•TY A unique hidden fastening system developed by Swan Secure Products (www.swansecure.com) is the EB•TY fastening system. The heart of the system is a plastic football shaped "biscuit" that fits into slots cut in the deck boards with a biscuit joiner (*see page 23*). The biscuit is inserted in a slot and secured with a screw. One of the big advantages to this system is all of the work is done from the top of the deck—this makes it particularly useful for low-lying decks where there is no clearance underneath.

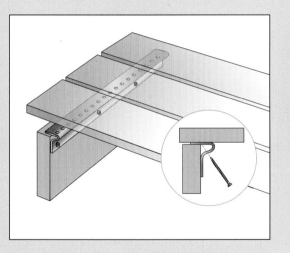

Brackets Another hidden system is a special metal bracket that attaches to the joists and provides a method for attaching the deck boards from underneath—leaving no fasteners exposed. The system *shown here* is manufactured by Grabber under the brand name Deckmaster (www.deckmaster.com). The brackets are available in either galvanized or stainless steel. This system works extremely well for raised decks with clearance below. On a low-lying deck with little or no clearance, you'll need to use a right-angle drill (*see page 22*) to drive in the screws.

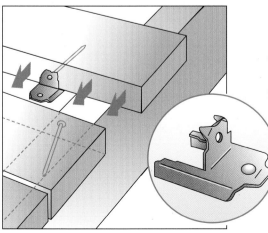

Deck clips Deck clips are another method of attaching deck boards without leaving fasteners exposed. The deck board ties *shown here* are manufactured by Simpson Strong-Tie and are installed with a single 10d nail. Locator prongs help position the clip for easier installation. Note that with all hidden fastening systems, it's imperative to check your local building code to make sure that they are allowed in your area.

Illustration based on original artwork © Simpson Strong-Tie, 2001

Fasteners: Screws

Galvanized and coated screws A relative newcomer to the fastener market, vinyl-coated screws come in two colors (tan and green) and are touted as weather-resistant. The screws are coated with a thin layer of vinyl, which seals the metal. This works great as long as the coating isn't disturbed. The problem is that when you drive the screw through a piece of wood, it rubs off the coating. I prefer stainless steel or hot-dipped galvanized screws, as their tougher coating doesn't wear off and they hold up better over time.

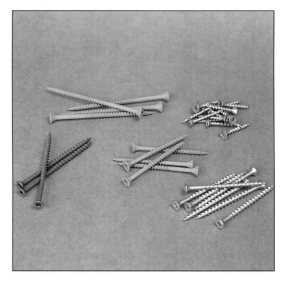

Bronze Silicone bronze screws have been popular in the boatbuilding trade for years because they stand up extremely well to the elements. When they're first made, they have the color of a fresh penny; but they'll oxidize and darken over time. This darker color makes silicone bronze an excellent choice for a Western cedar or red-wood deck, since the screws will blend right in as the deck ages.

Brass Brass screws have also been used in the boatbuilding trade for years, but they find less use in deck and porch construction. That's because brass is so soft, it tends to strip and/or break easily. If you do use brass screws, you can significantly reduce the risk of damage by first drilling the appropriate-sized pilot holes. You can further reduce screw-stripping friction by rubbing a little soap or paraffin on the threads before driving in the screw.

Fasteners: Nails

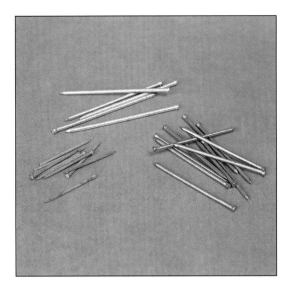

Galvanized Since nails used for deck and porch work are constantly exposed to the elements, they should be made from corrosion-resistant metals (like aluminum) or else galvanized to prevent rust. *Shown here* are galvanized casing and trim nails. Whichever type of galvanized nails you purchase, make sure that they're hot-dipped (not electroplated): Hot-dipped nails have been proven to hold up better over time.

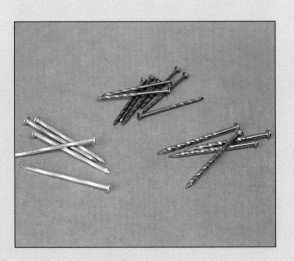

Spiral Whenever you need a nail with a bit of extra holding power, consider using a spiral nail (*see the photo at left*). These nails are sort of a hybrid between a nail and a screw. As they're driven into the wood, they twist and "screw" into the piece, gripping it better. Unfortunately, since the "threads" are so shallow, the gripping power is significantly less than that of a screw—but it's better than that of a straight-shank nail. Spiral nails can be found in corrosion-resistant metals such as aluminum and stainless steel, or they can be galvanized.

Framing nails Metal framing connectors are best attached with the manufacturer-recommended nails. The most common of these are joist nails (*see the photo at left*). These nails have a stout shank and increased shear strength. Please note that there are numerous sizes and types of nails for framing connectors. Your best bet is to use nails made by the manufacturer of the framing connector. Most lumberyards and home centers stock these right next to the connectors.

Framing Connectors

Metal framing connectors are designed for use on projects where you need to quickly attach parts together. The toughness of metal adds considerable rigidity and strength to any project.

Safety note: All framing connectors are rated to handle a maximum load. If you're not sure about which one to use, check with the manufacturer, a building contractor, or your building inspector.

Post bases

Post bases may be adjustable or nonadjustable. The adjustable type (*top in drawing*) offers moisture protection by lifting the post off the footing. This space also creates clearance for the washer and nut used to secure the post base to a footing via a J-bolt (*see page 32*). A slot in the bottom of the base allows you to slide it back and forth to fine-tune its position. The non-adjustable (fixed) base offers quick installation by inserting its prongs into the wet footing. The disadvantage here is that once the concrete sets up, you can't adjust its position.

Post caps

A post cap makes the transition from one framing member to another—quite often from post to beam. A pair of adjustable post caps can be spaced apart to fit a wide variety of framing situations. Retrofit post caps are also installed in pairs and are suitable for heavier loads than adjustable base caps.

Post stand-offs

A post stand-off is used underneath a column for a porch to lift up the column, thereby reducing decay. These stand-offs are attached to the end of the column prior to installation. For added rigidity, a rod embedded in the concrete passes up into the column through the stand-off.

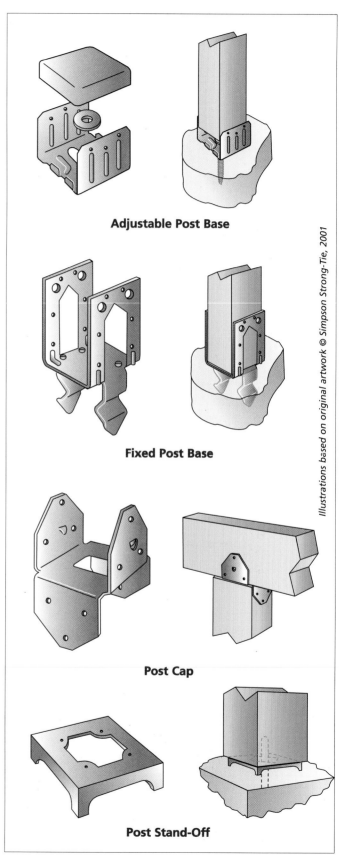

Adjustable Post Base

Fixed Post Base

Post Cap

Post Stand-Off

Illustrations based on original artwork © Simpson Strong-Tie, 2001

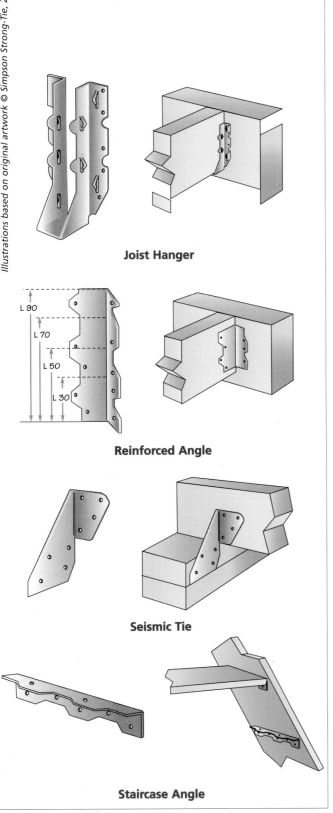

Joist Hanger

L 90

L 70

L 50

L 30

Reinforced Angle

Seismic Tie

Staircase Angle

Joist hangers

Joist hangers are by far the most used framing connector for decks and porches. They're designed to support a joist or other framing member from a post, beam, rim joist, header, etc. Joist hangers create a stronger joint than is possible by nailing framing members together.

Safety note: In order for joist hangers to be able to reliably support their designated load, they must be installed with special fasteners called joist hanger nails (*see page 29*).

Reinforcing angles

Many local building codes require reinforcing angles in numerous situations, such as where floor joists meet headers or rim joists, and where studs meet sole plates (*see the drawing at left*). Make sure to check with your local building inspector to identify what type of reinforcement (if any) is required in your area.

Seismic and hurricane ties

Originally developed for locations where seismic activity or a hurricane is a possibility, seismic and hurricane ties are designed to help hold a structure together during high winds and earthquakes (check to see whether they are required by code in your area). But it didn't take the construction industry long to find other uses for these—so much so that these ties are used regardless of location, often to attach field joists to a beam for a deck or porch.

Staircase angles

Staircase angles are a quick way to build a structurally sound staircase. They're attached to the stringer or carriage with joist hanger nails, and they support the treads.

Bolts

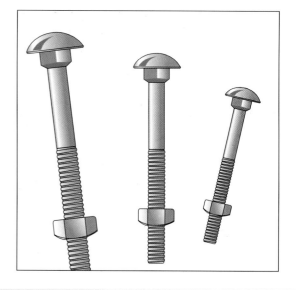

Carriage bolts A carriage bolt (also known as a carriage screw) is a large bolt that's partially threaded and features a smooth rounded head; *see the drawing at right.* Beneath the round head is a square shank that bites into the wood as a nut on the end of the bolt is tightened. These are particularly useful when access to one side of the bolt is limited and you won't be able to reach the head with a wrench. They're also often used when a more finished appearance is desired, as the rounded head is much less noticeable than a machine bolt.

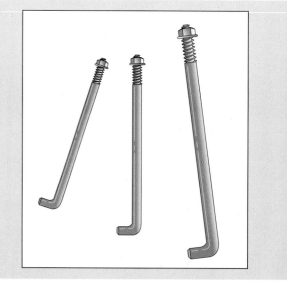

J-bolts A J-bolt is a headless machine bolt whose end is bent into a "J"; *see the drawing at right.* J-bolts are used extensively in deck and porch construction to secure post caps to concrete footings (*see page 44*). The bent end of the bolt is inserted into wet concrete and wiggled to release trapped air. It's important to push the bolt down far enough so the threaded end of the bolt fits under the base of the post cap. Once the concrete is set, the post cap is placed over the bolt and secured with a nut and washer.

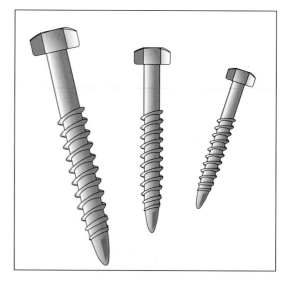

Lag bolts Lag bolts (also referred to as lag screws) are basically heavy-duty screws that are driven in with a wrench; *see the drawing at right.* Most are partially threaded, but shorter versions often have threads along the entire shank. Lag bolts offer a convenient way to secure parts together; but they do not offer the strength of a carriage bolt or machine bolt that runs completely through the parts and "clamps" them together via a washer and nut. Lag bolts are often used in conjunction with lag shields to secure a ledger to masonry (*see pages 55–56 for more on this*).

Ready-Made Parts

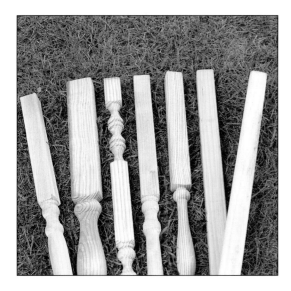

Balusters Of all the ready-made parts available for a deck or porch project, balusters come in the widest variety of shapes and sizes; *see the photo at left.* That's because manufacturers realize that every homeowner wants their deck or porch to be unique. With this is mind, you'll find square balusters and turned spindles in a variety of profiles and materials—most commonly pressure-treated pine and cedar. Turned spindles for porches can often be found pre-primed for easier finishing.

Posts As with balusters, you should be able to find posts in both pressure-treated pine and cedar, but with much fewer profile options. Most home centers carry one or two options. Note that if you're planning on using a simple square post, it may be less expensive to purchase 8' pieces and cut them to length yourself. A single 42"-long 4×4 cedar post can easily cost $20 to $30—you can make your own for less than $10 apiece. This can amount to considerable savings when you're looking to buy a set of posts for a railing (a standard deck will require around 10 posts).

Decorative caps You can spice up a plain post by adding one of many decorative caps available; *see the photo at left.* Caps can be square-cut, shaped, or turned from pressure-treated pine or cedar. Other varieties include pressed metal caps, and caps that combine metal and wood, like the copper-and-cedar cap *at right in the photo.* Finally, ingenious lighting manufacturers combine a low-voltage light with a decorative metal or vinyl fixture to provide both a visually interesting cap and lighting for the deck (*white fixture at top in the photo*).

Chapter 3
Basic Building Techniques

Whether you're planning on building a deck or a porch, there are a number of construction techniques common to both jobs. I'll start this chapter by taking you through the steps necessary to lay out, dig, and pour footings. The footings are a vital part of both projects because they transfer the weight of the project safely to the ground. The first thing you'll need to decide on is which of the two common types of footings to use: post above grade or post below grade (*opposite page*).

Once you've settled on a type of footing, the next step is to carefully lay out their locations. This involves building and installing temporary supports called batter boards to hold the mason's line that you'll use to define the rim joists (*pages 36–38*). After locating the footings, it's time to get out the shovel and dig the holes. Other, less labor-intensive options include renting a power auger or having the footing dug by a professional excavator; *see pages 39–41 for detailed step-by-step instructions.*

There's still a bit of heavy labor left—pouring the footings (*pages 42–43*). Even if you've never worked with concrete before, it's really quite simple since manufacturers started selling "ready-to-mix" concrete and concrete tube forms. Mixing concrete is just a matter of adding the correct amount of water to the dry mix. The only special tools you'll need are a wheelbarrow and a garden hoe or a mortar hoe. A mortar hoe works best—it looks just like an ordinary garden hoe except that there are a pair of large holes in the blade. These holes provide better mixing action as the hoe is drawn back and forth through the mixture. After the concrete is poured, you can add the post anchors (usually J-bolts) and post caps that will hold the posts (*pages 44–46*).

Then on to techniques for framing. Essential to any construction project are straight cuts in lumber. I've included a simple shop-made jig for your circular saw that makes super-accurate 45- and 90-degree cuts in boards up to and including 2×12s (*page 47*). Next, there's information on how to handle the inevitable warped board (*page 48*). Finally, on *page 49,* I'll cover how to work with composite deck boards.

Footing Options

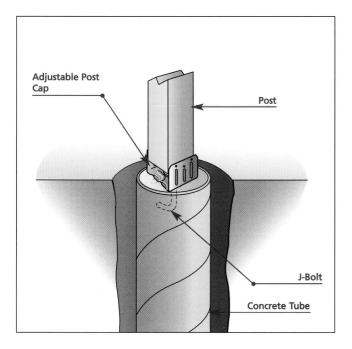

Adjustable Post Cap

Post

J-Bolt

Concrete Tube

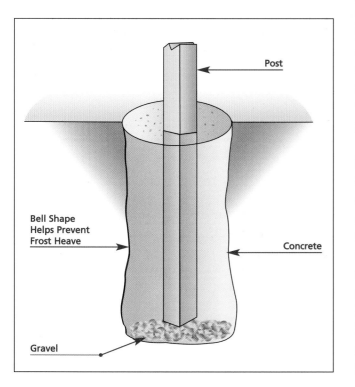

Post

Bell Shape Helps Prevent Frost Heave

Concrete

Gravel

When it's time to begin work on your new deck or porch, you'll need to decide which installation method to choose for the footings: post above grade, or post below grade.

Post above grade

Installing a post above grade is by far the most common way to add a footing. In this method, the post is installed in a metal framing connector called a post base cap. It 's secured to the concrete footing via a J-bolt; *see the drawing at left.* Since the J-bolt is embedded in the concrete, you get a solid connection.

The advantage to this system is twofold. First, since there's no wood contacting the ground, there's less chance of rot or insect damage (which can even happen if you use ground-contact-grade pressure-treated lumber). Second, if you use an adjustable post base cap (*see page 30*), you can make minor adjustments to the position of the post; this can be quite useful as the foundation is being built. The disadvantage to this method is that it requires more hardware (plus the time required to install it) than a post below grade does.

Post below grade

On a post below grade footing, the post itself is embedded in the concrete; *see the drawing at left.* Typically, the post rests on a bed of gravel to improve drainage. It's absolutely imperative to use ground-contact-grade pressure-treated wood for the post. Anything else will quickly deteriorate. Although a post-below-grade installation is the simplest method of adding a footing, it requires careful planning, positioning, and bracing of the post—you can't adjust the position of the post once the concrete sets up.

Locating Post Footings

The first step in building a deck or porch is to locate the footings that the posts and beam will rest on to support the rim and field joists. The number and location of the footings will vary from plan to plan. Check your plans to see where the footings need to be dug; in every case, footing locations are referenced off the ledger board. Although you can measure and carefully mark the intended location of the ledger board on the side of the house and reference off this, I recommend actually installing the ledger board (*see Step 1 below*). There are a few reasons for this, most of which are related to Murphy's Law, which states that if something can go wrong, it will. The last thing you want to do is dig and pour footings and them have to move them because of a problem encountered while installing the ledger board. To prevent this, it's best to install the ledger first and then use this as the reference point for locating the footings.

1 **Install ledger board** In a simple deck design, the footings support one-half the weight of the deck; the other half is supported by the ledger board that's attached to the house. Since all measurements for the deck are referenced off the ledger board, it's imperative that it be located and installed to properly support that weight. *See pages 52–54* for step-by-step directions on how to install a ledger board on a house with siding; *see page 55* for attaching a ledger to a brick or masonry exterior; and *see page 56* for attaching a ledger to stucco.

2 **Build batter boards** Batter boards are temporary supports made from scrap lumber that hold in place the mason's line that you'll use to locate the footings. For each batter board (you'll need two at each corner and one for each additional post along the perimeter), cut a pair of stakes from 1-by or 2-by scrap about 8" longer than the highest post. Make two angled cuts on the bottom of each stake to create a sharp point. Then cut a cross-piece about 2' long and attach it to the stakes with screws *as shown.*

3 **Position the boards** To position the batter boards, start by roughly locating the footings, using a tape measure. Then install a batter board about 2' past the footing. Pound the batter board into the ground with a sledgehammer until the stakes are roughly 6" into the ground. Install pairs of batter boards in the corners (*as shown*) and one at each post location around the perimeter.

4 **Run mason's line** Attach one end of a mason's line to the ledger at a post location. Then extend the line out until it meets the batter board and is roughly perpendicular to the ledger. Wrap it temporarily around the board, keeping the line taut. Next, use the 3-4-5 triangle method to check that the line is truly perpendicular to the ledger; *see the photo at left and the sidebar below*. Shift the line as needed until it's perpendicular. Then drive a nail into the batter board at the point (leaving about 2" exposed), and attach the line to the nail.

USING A 3-4-5 TRIANGLE

One of the oldest and most reliable ways to check to make sure reference lines are exactly perpendicular is to use a 3-4-5 triangle. To do this, start by measuring and marking a point 3 feet from the centerpoint where the lines cross (make this mark on either line). Then measure and mark 4 feet from the centerpoint on the adjacent line. Now measure the distance from the 3-foot mark to the 4-foot mark. If the lines are truly perpendicular, the distance will measure exactly 5 feet. If it doesn't, the lines aren't perpendicular and the position of one of the lines will have to be adjusted.

5 **Check lines for level** Attaching the mason's line to a protruding nail allows you to slide the nail up and down until it's perfectly level. The simplest way to check for this is to use a line level—a small level with hooks on each end that slip over the mason's line. Slide the level so that it's roughly in the center of the line, and shift the line up or down on the nail until it's level. Next, measure along the line to locate the centerpoint of the posts. Make a mark on the line, or flag it with a piece of tape. Repeat this for each footing.

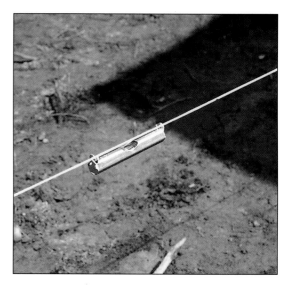

6 **Transfer location to ground** Once you've strung mason's line in each direction and have measured and marked the centerpoint of the posts on the line, you can transfer this location to the ground. The tool for the job here is a plumb bob. Position the string of the plumb bob directly over the crosspoints of the mason's line so that the bob hovers just slightly above the ground. As always, when using one of these, it's a good idea to have a helper on hand to steady the bob and mark its location.

7 **Mark location of footing** Now that you've located the footing, all that's left is to mark its position. There are a number of ways to do this, but the old "piece of scrap paper with a nail it in" still is the most common method used. Spray paint is another common practice, but a drawback of it is that it can be "erased" by an afternoon shower. Contractors often use highly visible orange plastic tape wrapped around a landscaping nail because it will hold up in bad weather and is easy to find.

Digging Footings

Digging and pouring footings are two of the most labor-intensive jobs of installing a deck or porch. If your budget allows it, I heartily recommend contracting out this heavy labor; *see page 41.* How deep you have to dig the footings will depend on the local frost line. Check with your local building inspector for the recommended footing depth, and have your local utility companies locate and mark underground electrical, gas, or water lines for you before you dig. (They'll be happy to do this for you.)

1 **Excavate** If you're manually digging the footings, start by breaking up the ground with a pickax. Then start excavating with a spade. As you dig down, you'll eventually need to switch to a post-hole digger to grab and pull out the dirt (*see page 23*). A popular alternative to this back-breaking manual digging is to rent a power auger from a local rental center. These beasts take some getting used to, and I recommend having plenty of muscular help to handle this powerful tool. Please note that if you live in a rocky region (as I do), a power auger is virtually useless for digging footings: When they hit a large rock, they basically stop and spin; you'll have to break out the shovels and prybars and go to work.

FORM OR NO FORM?

Footing without forms
The simplest method for creating a footing is to dig a hole and pour in cement—and either embed a post (*as shown below*) or install post base caps. The disadvantage to this method is that it tends to use a lot more concrete than is necessary to fill the hole. The advantages are you don't have to backfill and, if you make the base bell-shaped (*as shown*), it will firmly anchor the footing in the ground.

Footings using forms
Although a footing with a form requires a bit more work than not using one, it does have its advantages. The biggest is that the form accurately defines how much concrete you'll need. Most home centers have a chart that will tell you exactly how many bags of ready-mix concrete you'll need to fill a form regardless of its depth or diameter. The disadvantage: You have to cut and position the form as well as backfill after the concrete sets.

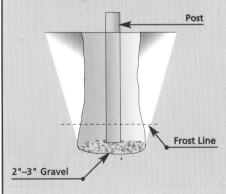

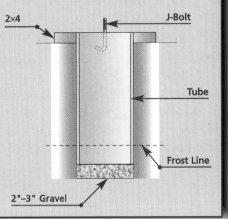

2 **Tamp bottom** Once you've dug the footings to the desired depth, the next step is to tamp the bottom with a store-bought tamper or a scrap of 4×4 (*as shown*). Tamping the bottom creates a flat, level, solid base for the gravel you'll add (*see Step 3*) and for the form (if you're using one). This is one of those often-skipped steps that can really make or break a footing. The footing is the foundation of the entire deck or porch, and it's worth the extra work now to make sure everything will turn out plumb and level.

3 **Add gravel for drainage** Regardless of whether you're using a form or not, you'll want to add a layer of gravel to the bottom of the hole to help water drain away from the footing; *see the photo at right.* Pour gravel into the hole and spread it around with a shovel so that it's flat and level. Continue adding gravel until you have a solid 2"- to 3"-thick layer.

4 **Prepare the forms** After you've established the depth of your footings, you can trim your forms (if applicable) to length. Add 2" to the hole depth and mark this length on your form. You can cut tube forms with a handsaw (*as shown*) or with a reciprocating saw and a long blade. It's important that these cuts be accurate, so it's best to mark the length all the way around the tube and to take your time as you make the cut.

HIRING AN EXCAVATOR

Depending on where you live and your budget, hiring an excavator to prepare your site and dig the footings may be an excellent investment. You might be surprised at how little an excavator will charge to do all or a portion of the work. Call around and get a couple of bids—sometimes all it takes is finding someone who's "hungry" for work.

The jobsite for one of the decks I built for this book was in a region that is known for its rocks. As a matter of fact,

the local contractors refer to the rocks as their "cash crop"—you can't sink a shovel more than an inch or two into the soil without hitting one. The site also had some small trees that needed to be removed and a rather serious drainage problem—the surrounding earth slanted toward the house, instead of away from it.

All three of these tasks would combine into a serious backache, so I called in a local excavator. In about three hours, he had removed the trees and shrubs, leveled and sloped the soil away from the house, and dug the footings. I couldn't believe the size of the rocks he pulled out with his backhoe (some larger than its bucket!). An item to note when working with an excavator. First, if you have trees to be removed, cut them down (or have them cut down in advance), but

leave about 12" to 14" of stump exposed. This provides a "handle" for the blade or bucket to grab onto to assist in their removal.

Pouring Footings

As I mentioned earlier, pouring footings is hard work. The tough part isn't the actual pouring, it's lugging the bags of concrete around. Although a typical bag weighs only 60 pounds, when you need 14 bags (as I did for the footings for this deck), it adds up (over 800 pounds). Still, this doesn't sound too overwhelming until you begin to think about how many times you have to move it. Load it into your cart at the home center, transfer it into your car or truck, unload it at the job site, lift it into the wheelbarrow to mix it, and transport it to the footings via a wheelbarrow. It's easily conceivable that you'll lift each bag five or more times. All of a sudden 800 pounds turns into 2 tons (oh, my aching back). If your budget allows and there's a nearby concrete company, consider purchasing your concrete ready-mixed. Just make real sure before these guys show up that (1) you order the correct amount of concrete, (2) your forms are in place, and (3) the forms have been inspected (if applicable). If they have to wait, the meter's running.

1 **Position the forms** If you're using tube forms (*as shown here*), you'll need to position them in the footing holes so they're level and plumb, and then lock them in place so they don't move as the concrete is poured. Cut a pair of 2×4 scraps to span the hole, and then butt them up against the form, checking to make sure that the form is plumb. Screw each side of the form to one of the 2×4s. If the site is sloped, drive a stake or two into the ground next to the 2×4s and screw these to the 2×4s to prevent them from moving.

2 **Mix the concrete** If you have only two or three footings to pour, it's easy enough to mix your own concrete. You'll need ready-to-mix concrete (typically available in 60-pound bags), a wheelbarrow, a hoe (preferably a mortar hoe), and water. Dump a bag of concrete mix in the wheelbarrow, and form a depression in the middle to hold the water. Carefully measure the recommended amount and pour it into the depression. Work the mix and water back and forth with the hoe until the concrete is fully mixed.

3 **Pour the footing** Depending on how agile you are with a wheelbarrow, you may or may not want to try pouring the concrete into the hole by tipping it up and sliding the concrete into the hole. If you're not feeling adventurous, you can simply drop the concrete in the form one shovelful at a time (*as shown here*). This may take longer, but it's usually more reliable—and less messy.

4 **Displace bubbles** As you pour the concrete into the form or hole, you'll inevitably create air pockets in the concrete. To get rid of these, use a scrap of wood to periodically poke or stir the concrete (*see the photo at left*). Alternatively, you can tamp the concrete with a 2×4 or 4×4. It's best to do this periodically—after you've poured 12" of concrete or so. Note: Since the concrete will likely settle a bit, it's best to overfill it slightly—you'll screed off any excess in the next step.

5 **Screed to level** Once the form or post hole is filled and you've allowed it to settle for about 15 minutes, it's time to level the concrete. For a footing with forms, this is simplicity itself. Take a scrap of 2×4 that's longer than the diameter of the form and pull it across the top of the form, using a sawing motion—this is referred to by masons as *screeding*. Footings without forms can also be leveled with a scrap 2×4—they just require constant checking with a level.

Installing Post Anchors

Once your footings have been poured and leveled, the next step is to install the post anchors (for adjustable post base caps) or the post base caps themselves if they're nonadjustable. In order to transfer the load of the deck or porch evenly to the footing, the post base cap and post anchor should be centered on the footing and be plumb and level. As the most typical form of post anchors is the J-bolt (*see page 32*), I'll take you through the steps necessary to install one here. This installation method can also be used for installing a one-piece nonadjustable post base cap (*see page 30*); you'll just need to skip to the instructions for installing post base caps (*on page 46*) as soon as you've inserted the prongs of the cap in the concrete. Whichever you use, an anchor or a nonadjustable cap, you'll first need to reinstall your batter boards, restring the mason's line, and make sure the lines are parallel and/or perpendicular to the ledger board. You'll need these to accurately locate the centerpoints for the anchors (*Step 1 below*).

1 **Locate anchors** Just as you did when you located the posts prior to digging the footings (*pages 36–39*), you'll need to repeat this task to locate the exact point for inserting the post anchors. Here again, the plumb bob is the tool for the job. Hold the string so that it butts up against (but doesn't deflect) the point where the strings meet. Hold the plumb bob steady until the bob stops moving about ¼" above the surface of the concrete. When it's motionless, carefully allow the point to mark the center in the concrete.

2 **Insert and set** Now that you've located the insertion point, you can install the post anchor. For a J-bolt, hold it at an angle (*as shown*), and start by inserting the curved end of the J into the concrete at the centerpoint. Once the head of the J is embedded, tilt the bolt up gradually until it's vertical as you press it further into the concrete. Continue pushing down (and wiggling slightly to prevent air pockets from forming) until the desired amount of bolt is exposed (check your post base cap for proper clearance).

3 **Recheck the position** Once you've fully inserted the post anchor, it's important to check its position one more time. It's surprisingly easy for it to end up considerably off-center—even when you're careful. Use the plumb bob, as you did to locate the insertion point, to make sure it's where it should be. Adjust the position of the anchor as necessary.

4 **Check for level** Finally, check to make sure that the post anchor is plumb and level. The simplest way to do this is to press a torpedo level or a straight scrap of wood up against the bolt to force the bolt into a perfectly vertical position. Work the level or scrap of wood all the way around the bolt so that you'll be sure it isn't tilted. Don't simply align this by eye—take this extra step to make sure it's straight.

5 **Backfill after inspection** At this point, you can allow the concrete to set up. After it's set, you'll most likely need to call in a building inspector to check the footing before you backfill. Warning: If you backfill prior to inspection, the inspector will make you dig it up so that he or she can inspect it! Avoid this common mistake by scheduling a footing inspection early on in the project.

Installing Post Caps

1 **Mark reference line** After the post anchors have been installed and the concrete has had ample opportunity to set up, you can install the post caps. The important thing here is that the post caps end up parallel to the ledger. The simplest way to ensure this (assuming the post anchors were located and installed properly) is to lay a straight, long board across two or more of the footings so that the board butts up against the post anchors, *as shown.* Then trace along the edge of the board to establish a reference point.

2 **Position the post cap** If you're using an adjustable post base cap, position it on the footing so that it's centered on the post anchor. Slide the post cap around until its front and back edges are roughly parallel to the line you marked in Step 1. Then butt the corner of a try square or framing square up against the edge of the cap, with one edge flush with the marked reference line, and check to make sure that it is, in fact, parallel.

3 **Tighten** Holding the post base cap firmly in place, slip the washer that came with the J-bolt over the bolt, and thread the nut in place. Note: To prevent the post base cap from "creeping" once it's secured, it's important that you install a washer under the nut. Tighten the nut with a socket wrench and then double-check the position of the post base cap to make sure it didn't move.

Straight Cuts in Lumber

Just as with any construction or framing project, it's important that all your cuts be accurate. For most deck and porch jobs, you'll primarily be making 90-degree and 45-degree cuts. Power miter saws work great for these, but most can only cut through a 2×6 in one pass. This is great for deck boards, but how do you cut wider stock,

like the 2×8 joists or 2×10 beams? The answer: a circular-saw jig like the one *shown in the photo at left.* Although you can purchase a number of saw guides, you can save yourself some money by making your own; *see the sidebar below.*

The advantage of the jig *shown here* is that the edge of the jig (for both 90- and 45-degree cuts) indicates the cut line. That means all you have to do is mark the board for length, slide the jig over until the edge aligns with the mark (with the front cleat pressed up against the board), and then make the cut. There's no need to draw reference lines.

CIRCULAR-SAW JIG

The circular-saw jig consists of a 1/4" hardboard base, two 1/4" hardboard edge guides, and a pair of 3/4"-thick hardwood cleats. To make the jig, start by cutting the base to size. In order to crosscut a 2×12, make the base 13" wide—11 1/2" for the 2×12, and 1 1/2" for the two cleats. The length will depend on your saw base. In most cases, 24" will do. Then cut two hardwood cleats to this same length and screw them to the base.

To guide the saw to make a perfect 45- or 90-degree cut, the next step is to add two 2"-wide guide strips cut from 1/4" hardboard. These are simply glued to the base. To position the straight guide, measure the distance from the base of your saw to the saw blade and add 1/2". Transfer this measurement to the base and make a line. Then carefully align the strip with this line and clamp it in place, making sure that it's perfectly perpendicular to the front

edge of the base. (Note: You'll need to cut the top end at 45 degrees before gluing it in place.)

Now cut a 45-degree miter on one end of the 45-degree strip, apply glue, and butt it up against the straight guide so that it continues the 45-degree miter you cut on its end. Here again, check that this guide is perfectly 45 degrees to the front edge before applying clamps. After the glue has dried, place the circular saw base against each guide in turn and make a full cut. This trims the base, leaving a crisp edge that defines the cut line.

Straightening Deck Boards

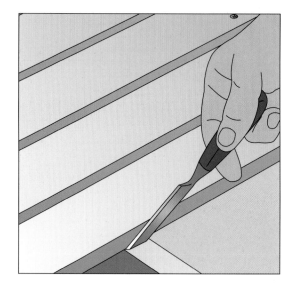

Chisel as a prybar One of the simplest ways to persuade a warped deck board to straighten out is to use a chisel as a prybar. To do this, butt the flat side of the chisel up against the board to be adjusted, directly over a joist. Then drive the chisel into the joist about ¼" deep with a hammer. Now you can leverage the board over by moving the handle of the chisel toward the board. If the board is really warped, try driving the chisel in at an angle (*as shown*) for added leverage.

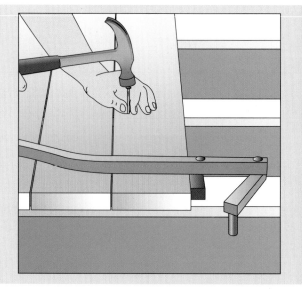

Deck straightener The folks at Cepco Tools (Website www.cepcotool.com) make a nifty deck-board straightener called the Bowrench; *see the drawing at right.* The best thing about this tool is that once you've used it to straighten a board, you can let it go and it will hold the board in place while you secure it. The leverage action is so strong with this tool that you can even straighten several boards at once. The manufacturer also offers an adapter for installing tongue-and-groove flooring.

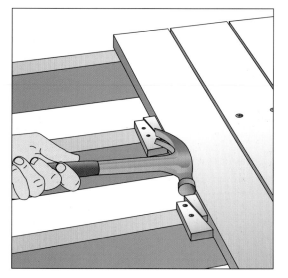

Scrap-wood wedges Although the scrap-wood wedge method of board straightening can be time-consuming, it's very effective and it frees up your hands to secure the deck boards. All you need are a couple of scrap-wood wedges, some screws, and a hammer. Screw one wedge to the joist, and then insert the other so the wedge angles are opposing. Then drive in the loose wedge with a hammer until the board straightens (*see the drawing at right*). After you've secured the deck board, remove the wedges and continue installing boards.

Working with Composite Materials

Cutting Virtually all of the composite decking materials can be cut with the same tools used to cut wood decking. As with any crosscut, you'll get a smoother cut by using a fine-tooth carbide-tipped blade. A standard 40-tooth combination blade will work fine. With pure plastic decking, I recommend a 60-tooth blade since these brittle materials have a tendency to chip-out. Because the plastic in the composites will melt if you use too slow a cut rate, it's best to keep the blade moving along at all times.

Screws are self-sealing One of the niftiest things about plastic-and-wood composite decking is that the screws "self-seal" as they are installed—that is, the friction that the screw generates as it is driven in will temporarily melt the plastic around it. Once the screw is in place, the plastic flows back around it, effectively encasing it and sealing out moisture. What a great way to prevent corrosion!

Not for the foundation It's important to note that virtually every composite deck board available on the market is intended only for use as decking. This stuff is not engineered to support loads and should never be used to build a foundation. "If it's good for the deck, it'd be great for the foundation" does not apply here. See the chart on *page 24* for guidelines for supporting composite decking.

Chapter 4

Building a Basic Deck

Building a deck is an exciting and rewarding home improvement job. The rewards are immediate: increased living space and a place to enjoy the outdoors. Over the years, I've built a lot of decks, and the best piece of advice I can give you is to not hurry the process. I can't overemphasize the importance of taking your time in the initial phases of building a deck—particularly installing the ledger and the footings. Any mistakes here will be multiplied as the construction progresses.

Also, don't forget to work with your local building inspector not only in the planning stages, but also during the construction. Make sure to schedule the necessary inspections in advance to prevent having to redo work (like digging out the foundations because they weren't inspected before you backfilled them).

I'll start this chapter by going over the necessary steps in preparing the site (*opposite page*), then jump immediately into how to install the ledger. I'll take you through installing a ledger on a sided exterior (the most common kind) one step at a time—everything from cutting away siding to create a flat surface for the ledger, to caulking the bolt holes to prevent water damage (*pages 52–54*). If your exterior is brick or stucco,

there are instructions on how to install a ledger on these, on *pages 55 and 56, respectively.*

Once the ledger is in place, you can create the footings (*see Chapter 3*) and then install the posts (*page 57*) and beams (*pages 58–59*) that support the joists. Then for the fun part: adding the joists. I'll cover using joist hangers, installing rim joists and field joists, how to strengthen the corner joints, and how to lock in the field joists, all on *pages 60–62*.

With the foundation installed, the deck is finally beginning to take shape. Adding the deck boards is the next step. On *pages 63–64*, I'll show you how to install traditional wood deck boards, including some tips on how to prevent them from splitting as they're installed and how to keep them looking good over time. If you're planning on laying down composite decking, there's advice on how to do this (*pages 65–66*). Finally, I've included tips on trimming out the deck, including adding fascia or end caps, *on page 67.*

Site Preparation

1 **Level the site** The first step in building a deck or porch is to prepare the ground at the site. If the soil slants toward the house, instead of away from it as it should for proper drainage, bring in an excavator to level and then slope the ground as necessary (*see the photo at left*). This is also the time to remove any trees, shrubs, or plants that will get in the way of the project.

2 **Lay moisture barrier** To prevent plants from growing under the deck or porch and to provide a barrier to moisture, it's a good idea to lay down a layer of 4-mil plastic. The type used for vapor barriers in house construction works great for this. If moisture isn't a concern and you just want to prevent things from growing, you can lay down landscape cloth. Note that many types of composite decking (especially the extruded types) will buckle and warp if there's a lot of moisture underneath; you should definitely install a plastic barrier if you intend to use one of these.

3 **Add gravel** Regardless of whether you lay down landscape cloth or plastic, it will stay down better over the years if you weigh it down with some loose gravel. Empty some bags of gravel evenly across the plastic or landscape cloth, and spread it out with a shovel, rake, or hoe. Be careful not to tear the fabric or plastic, and concentrate the gravel at the edges. It's best to completely cover the edges so that wind can't slip underneath and lift them up and/or create air pockets.

Installing the Ledger

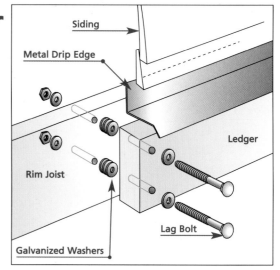

Siding

Metal Drip Edge

Rim Joist

Galvanized Washers

Ledger

Lag Bolt

Aside from the footings (*see Chapter 3*), the ledger is the most important structural part of a solid foundation. The ledger is simply a stout board—typically 2×10 pressure-treated lumber—that's fastened securely to the house. The challenge is attaching it securely while making sure that moisture doesn't get trapped between the ledger and the house. A metal drip edge helps to funnel moisture away, and galvanized washers inserted between the ledger and house provide drainage; *see the drawing at right.*

1 **Draw outline on house and cut siding** The first step to installing a ledger is to locate its position on the house and remove any siding (if applicable). Refer to your deck design for placement, and draw the outline of the ledger on the house—a chalk line works best for this. Then set the blade of a circular saw to just cut through the siding and make four plunge cuts, stopping just short of the corners. **Warning:** Don't even think about bolting a ledger directly to the siding. It will end up crooked and will not support the weight of the deck—this is a disaster waiting to happen.

2 **Square up corners** In most cases, you'll be able to easily pry off the siding after you've made the plunge cuts in Step 1. If the siding won't come off, finish cutting through the siding with a chisel. Then remove the siding and square up the corners with a chisel, *as shown in the photo at right.* Use a sharp chisel and take light cuts, as the siding is most likely not supported by a wall stud; if you apply too much force, the siding can easily crack.

3 **Measure and cut ledger** With the outline marked on the house and the siding removed, you can measure and cut the ledger to length; consult your plans for the correct length. Note that most ledgers are 3" shorter than the overall width (length) of the deck to allow the rim joists to be nailed directly to their ends; *refer to the deck anatomy drawing on page 11.* Cut the ledger with a circular saw, and take the time to make a square cut (consider making and using the jig shown on *page 47*).

4 **Lay out joists** Although you can lay out the locations for the field joists after the ledger has been installed, it's a whole lot easier to do it now. Lay the ledger on a couple of sawhorses, and carefully measure and mark the locations of the joists. Consult your deck plans for this, and use a speed square (*as shown*) or a combination square to lay out these locations accurately. Make a large X to indicate which side of the marked line the joist is to be installed on.

5 **Install flashing** The flashing that directs moisture away from the ledger is installed by slipping it up under the siding. You'll have the best access now for this, before the ledger is installed. Measure and mark a piece of flashing (commonly referred to as drip edge), and trim it to length with a pair of metal snips. Depending on your siding, you may need to remove a few nails to allow the flashing to slip fully up under the siding. I like to apply a bead of silicone caulk to the top edge of flashing before slipping it in—this helps hold it in place and creates a good seal.

6 **Drill holes for bolts** Refer to your deck plans for recommended locations for bolting the ledger to the house. In most cases, pairs of bolts are spaced every 24", starting about 6" in from one end. The best way I've found to drill the mounting holes is to first drill the holes in the ledger (*see the photo at right*) and then use the ledger as a template to drill the holes in the house—typically into its rim joists (*see the inset photo*). The easiest way to hold the ledger in position is to temporarily screw it to the house with a couple of 3" deck screws.

7 **Seal holes with caulk** For the neverending battle to prevent moisture damage, I recommend squirting a shot of silicone caulk in each bolt hole before installing the bolts. This keeps water from traveling along the threads of the bolt and into the rim joists of your home. One full ratchet of a caulk gun will seal the bolt nicely. More is not better here, though, since excess caulk will simply pour out the other end (in the case of through bolts) or be forced out (in the case of lag bolts) as you tighten the bolt.

8 **Tighten nuts** Remove the screws you installed to temporarily hold the ledger in place, and insert bolts in each hole. Then slip three galvanized washers onto each bolt and lift the ledger up into position. Have a helper assist you in lining up all the bolts with the holes in the house. This balancing act is worth the effort to get those washers between the ledger and the house. Once they're in place, tighten each bolt to secure the ledger. Note: If you're using lag screws, take care not to over-tighten, as they have a tendency to strip out.

Masonry Ledgers

1 **Drill holes with a hammer drill** Attaching a ledger to a home that has a brick exterior is fairly straightforward. Follow the instructions on *pages 52–54* to install the ledger, except skip steps 2 and 3. When it comes time to locate the ledger on the house, try to adjust the position of the ledger or mounting holes so that you'll be drilling into the bricks and not into the mortar (this is best done with a hammer drill and a masonry bit, *as shown*). Note: The holes are sized to accept lag shields; consult your plans for the proper size.

2 **Install lag shields** The lag bolts that you'll use to secure the ledger to the house are driven into lag shields—round metal fasteners that expand as the bolt enters to grip the sides of the hole. In most cases, you'll need to drive the lag shield into the hole with a hammer. If the hole is sized properly for the lag shield, this won't take a lot of force. Too much force and it's easy to fracture or damage the shield because they're most often made from soft lead.

3 **Attach ledger** After you've installed the lag shields, you can install the ledger. Here again, it's best to slip three galvanized washers onto each bolt to create a drainage space between the ledger and the house. Also, don't forget to seal out moisture with a shot of silicone caulk (*see page 54*). Finally, as when installing any lag bolt, take care not to overtighten the bolt—it's really easy to strip out a lag shield.

Stucco Ledgers

1 **Draw outline** Attaching a ledger to a stucco exterior is similar to attaching one to a brick exterior (*see page 55*). The major differences are how you drill through the wall and what you'll hit; *see steps 2 and 3 below.* As when installing any ledger, the first step is to locate its position on the house and trace its outline. Since you can't temporarily attach the ledger to the house with screws as you did for a sided exterior, the next best thing is to support it from underneath with cleats (*see the photo at right*).

2 **Drill through ledger into wall** Just as you'd do with a sided or brick exterior, drill the mounting holes in the ledger first and then use it as a template to locate the holes in the exterior wall. For best results when drilling into stucco (which has a tendency to crack easily), use a very sharp carbide-tipped masonry bit, a high speed, and a slow feed rate. I don't recommend using a hammer drill—the percussion it provides can be too much for the delicate covering.

3 **Attach with lag screws** The fragility of stucco also comes into play when it's time to attach the ledger. Obviously, overtightening the lag bolts can cause damage. Take it easy as you snug up the bolts, and give them only a quarter-turn or so past friction-tight. As always, apply a shot of silicone caulk before inserting the bolt, and don't forget to add the galvanized washers (*see page 52*) to provide drainage to prevent moisture damage.

Adding the Posts

1 **Set in anchors** Once the ledger is in place, you can lay out, dig, and pour the footings (*see pages 36–43*). After the footings are in and the post anchors and post caps are installed (*see pages 44–46*), you can install the posts. Start by cutting the posts to a rough length (about 4" longer than required). Then place each post in the post cap *as shown in the photo at left.* Note: It's a good idea to brush a coat of preservative onto the bottom of the post to retard moisture damage or rot.

2 **Plumb the post** The next step is to make sure the post is plumb and then temporarily secure it in place so that you can fasten it to the post caps (*Step 3*). Start by pounding a stake into the ground on two adjacent sides of the post. Then screw a scrap-wood brace to each cleat. Now you can use a level to plumb the post. When the post checks out in both directions, secure each brace to the post with screws, *as shown.*

3 **Attach post to post cap** Now that the post is plumb, it can be permanently attached to the post cap that it rests in. Make sure to use the galvanized nails recommended by the framing connector manufacturer. Since this is such an important connection, I like to drive nails into all of the predrilled holes in the post cap. Be careful as you do this because hammering can shift the post out of position. Check the post frequently with a level, or avoid the problem entirely by first securing the post with a screw on each side (they won't cause the post to shift) and then hammer in nails.

Installing the Beams

1 **Attach rim joist** How you install the beams will depend on how they attach to the posts. For beams that rest directly on the post, you'll need to use a water level to transfer the ledger position on the post and then cut the post to length. For beams that attach to the sides of the post (*as shown here*), start by temporarily attaching the rim joists to the post. This allows you to butt the beam up under the rim joists (*see Step 2*). Attach each rim joist to the ledger and the post with a single 3" deck screw.

2 **Position beam** With the rim joists in place, you can now position the beams one at a time by lifting each up under the rim joists and temporarily screwing it to the end posts by driving a single 3" deck screw into each post. Use a 4' level to make sure the beam is level before temporarily attaching it; *see the photo at right.* A helper is invaluable here because each beam is most likely a long and very heavy pressure-treated 2×10 or 2×12.

3 **Drill countersinks** Depending on where your beam is located—whether the decking is cantilevered or not—will have an impact on whether or not you need to countersink the bolt holes. If the decking does extend out past the beam, you don't have to worry about exposed bolt heads. If the beam is flush with the end of the deck or it'll be covered with fascia, you may want to recess the bolts to prevent them from catching on a child's arm or a piece of clothing. If you're planning on recessing the bolts, lay out and drill the countersinks now; *see the photo at right.*

4 **Attach the posts** If you've drilled countersinks, simply drill a hole in the center of each for a bolt. If you didn't countersink, lay out and drill the holes. As you'll likely need to drill through 7" or more of material, use an extra-long drill bit (available individually or in sets), usually in stock at most hardware stores and home centers. Just remember to back the bit out often and clear the flutes to prevent clogs. Then insert the bolts (*see the photo at left*), add washers and nuts, and tighten with a socket wrench (*inset*). Here again, silicone in the bolt holes will prevent water damage.

5 **Cut the posts level** Now that the beams have been attached to the posts, you can trim the posts level with the beams. There are a couple of ways to do this. A reciprocating saw fitted with a long blade will make quick work of this—just make sure that you don't cut into the beams. The method I prefer takes a little more elbow grease but is less likely to damage the beams: I lay a handsaw flat on the beams and use them to guide the blade as I cut through the post (*see the photo at left*).

6 **Caulk bolt heads** Even though you sealed the bolts before you installed them, it's best to dab a bit of silicone caulk onto the bolt heads to further help keep moisture out. I like to apply caulk to both the head and the exposed threads of the bolt. This not only helps prevent rot, but it also keeps the galvanized nuts and bolts dry—dry bolts won't rust and discolor the wood.

Attaching the Joists

With the ledger in place and the footings, posts, and beams installed, you're finally ready to "build" the deck. From this point on, the work will go surprisingly quickly—especially if you were careful when installing the ledger and footings. One of the things that helps speed up the construction of the foundation is the joist hanger. Joist hangers are easy to install and do a terrific job of supporting joists; *see steps 1 and 2 below.* One of the decisions you'll have to make concerning joist hangers is whether or not to use them to support the field joists on both the ledger and the rim joist that's opposite and parallel to the ledger. In my opinion, they're really not necessary on the rim joist. I prefer to screw the rim joist directly to the field joists and secure the field joists to the beam with a special metal brace called a hurricane tie (*see Step 7 on page 62*). Refer to your plans and consult with your local building inspector for the recommended method of attachment.

1 **Position joist hangers** Attaching joist hangers is really a two-step process. Step 1 is to align one vertical inside edge of a hanger with one of the layout lines you scribed on the ledger before it was installed (*Step 4 on page 53*). With the opening of the hanger spanning the X mark you made, place a scrap of joist material in the hanger. Then move the hanger up and down along the line until the top of the scrap is flush with the top of the ledger. Now secure the aligned side with joist hanger nails (*see the photo at right*).

2 **Install joist hangers** Step 2 is to squeeze the loose side of the hanger up against the scrap block and the attached side to create the perfect slot for a joist. Once in place, secure the remaining side with joist hanger nails (*see the photo at right*). Note that some joist hangers are designed for longer nails that pass through the hanger at a steep angle to crisscross and effectively "lock" the hanger in place on the ledger or rim joist.

3 **Check for square** Once all the joist hangers are in place along the ledger, I like to add the two rim joists that will define the sides, or ends, of the deck. These joists don't fit into joist hangers; instead they are screwed directly to the side of the ledger with three or more 3" deck screws. Set each rim joist in place and attach it to the ledger. Next, use the 3-4-5 triangle (*see page 37*) to pivot each rim joist until it's perfectly perpendicular to the ledger (*see the photo at left*). Toenail the rim joists to the beam to hold them in place.

4 **Add field joists** With the rim joists in place and aligned, you can measure and mark the field joist locations on the beam. Here again, make a mark to define one edge of the joist and draw an X to indicate which side of the line to install the joist on. Measure and cut the field joists to length, and set one in each joist hanger so the other end aligns with the marks you made on the beam. Give each joist a tap or two on the end with a hammer to seat it fully in the joist hanger, and secure it to the joist hanger with nails.

5 **Secure final rim joist** At this point I like to attach the final rim joist that runs parallel to the ledger. Because this joist is usually long and heavy (as in the case of the 16' 2×8 *shown here*), have a helper on hand to position and secure it. Start by securing the ends to the side rim joists with 3" deck screws. Then, making sure each field joist is still aligned with the marks on the beam, secure the rim joist to each field joist with 3" deck screws. Alternatively, you could install joist hangers on the rim joist.

6 **Add corner braces** Whenever I can, I like to add metal braces to help strengthen the butt joints of a deck wherever there isn't a joist hanger. This is especially true for the corners of a deck, where the rim joists and/or ledger are just held together with screws. Metal corner braces like the one *shown in the photo* are quick and easy to install and will add rigidity and longevity to your deck or porch foundation. If possible, fill each of the predrilled holes with joist hanger nails for optimum support.

7 **Add hurricane ties** Adding metal braces also applies to the field joists. There's a special brace often referred to as a hurricane tie that, although developed to help hold structures together during hurricanes, has found wide acceptance in all parts of the country. One face of a hurricane tie is nailed to the beam, the other to the field joist (*see the photo at right*). This helps secure the joist and prevents it from moving or "creeping" over time.

8 **Add blocking if required** In some areas of the country, your local code may require blocking. Blocking is just short lengths of joist material that are attached between the joists to prevent the joists from twisting (*see the photo at right*). Blocking may also be necessary if you're using one of the complex decking patterns (*see pages 12–13*). The blocking in this case is designed to both support the deck boards and provide a nailing surface.

Installing Wood Deck Boards

1 **Position first board** To install wood deck boards, start at the ledger and work out toward the end (some composites require the opposite approach; *see page 65*). Measure, mark, and cut the first deck board to length and place it next to the house. Don't worry about aligning the end of the board; allow it to "run wild"—you'll trim it later. To provide clearance for drainage, I space the board about ½" from the exterior. A couple of extra ½" bolts come in handy as spacers; *see the photo at left.*

2 **Attach to joists** I always recommend screws when it comes time to attach deck boards. Sure, nails are faster, but they just don't have the holding power that screws offer. Note: An autofeed screwgun (like the one shown on *page 23*) can actually install a screw faster than you can hammer in a nail. Depending on the material (like ipe; *see page 25*), you may need to drill pilot holes. Regardless of the material, it's always a good idea to drill pilot holes near the end of the board to prevent splitting (*inset*).

3 **Establish gap** How big the gap should be between the deck boards (if any) will depend on the material you use. The standard for years was to insert 16d nails between boards, *as shown in the photo.* This might look nice when the deck is laid, but if you're using pressure-treated wood, it will likely shrink considerably over time. You best bet here is to butt the boards up against each other and fasten them to the joists. If you're using a composite, consult the manufacturer's installation instructions for the recommended gap.

4 **Check for parallel** Here's a trick that the pros use to keep deck boards aligned as they install them. Although you might not think it's necessary to check to make sure the boards are going down properly (they are, after all, the same width, yes?), you'd be surprised at the inconsistencies in some deck boards (either wood or composite). After you've installed four or five boards, stop and measure from the ledger to the edge of the boards at both ends. If there's a discrepancy, adjust the gap width of the next boards you install to correct it.

5 **Trim the "wild" ends** Once all the deck boards are in place, you can tidy up any overhanging or "wild" ends by trimming them all at once. Consult your plans for the proper overhang (if any), and measure and mark a cut line (the best way to do this is to snap a chalk line). Then use a circular saw to carefully remove the wild ends—and make sure to cut on the waste side of the line (*see the photo at right*). Finish off the cuts near the ledger, using a handsaw or a reciprocating saw.

6 **Coat ends with preservative** After you've cut the deck boards to final length, it's a good idea to "treat" the ends of the cut lumber with a preservative. Why treat treated lumber? Because even under pressure, the treatment often doesn't penetrate all the way to the center of the board. As soon as you cut it, you may expose untreated wood. At most home centers you can usually find a preservative similar to that which was used to treat the lumber. Brush on a generous coat or two, *as shown in the photo at right.*

Installing Composite Decking

1 **Install starter strip** Solid composite decking goes down much like solid wood. Extruded structural composites (like the TimberTech decking *shown here*) require a specific sequence. Tongue-and-groove products usually have a "starter strip"—a narrow piece with a groove to accept the first board. Since you'll likely need to rip a final board to width, it's best to place that against the house so it will be less visible. With this in mind, install the starter strip on the rim joist and work back toward the house.

2 **Install planks** Once the starter strip is in place, you can begin installing the planks. Since many composites are fragile until installed, always carry them on edge with at least two people to support each end. Use hand pressure only to slip the tongue of each plank into the groove. Drive a 2½" stainless steel screw through the lip below the groove at an angle into the joist. For best results, start fastening in the middle of the plank and work out toward the ends. Leave a ³⁄₁₆" gap between boards laid end to end and between fascia boards and planks.

3 **Face-screw final plank** When all the full-width planks have been installed, you'll likely need to trim the final piece to fit against the house. Carefully measure, mark, and cut this piece to width, making sure to leave a ³⁄₁₆" gap between the plank and the house. To fully support the plank, you may need to install a cleat under the unsupported end; see the installation instructions for more on this. Since you won't have clearance to drive the final screws in at an angle, the last piece is screwed through the face into the ledger; *see the photo at left.*

4 Trim wild ends Just as you would when installing any other deck board, it's best to allow composite deck boards to "run wild" instead of trying to align them with the rim joists. To trim them to length, measure and mark the cut by snapping a chalk line. Use a circular saw to carefully trim the excess off, making sure to cut on the waste side of the line.

5 Attach end caps Unlike solid composites, which leave a clean edge when cut, an extruded structural composite leaves an edge that needs to be covered for best appearance. One way to handle this is to install fascia boards; *see Step 6 below.* Another method offered by some manufacturers is end caps. These are thin strips of the same material used for the deck boards and are typically screwed to the ends of the boards *as shown here.* Solid-plastic end caps often have clips that allow you to snap them in place.

6 Or, attach fascia I prefer covering the ends of composites with fascia (*as shown here*) since I usually want to cover the pressure-treated foundation anyway. Composite fascia is attached to the rim joists every 3' or so. Please note that virtually every composite fascia board manufactured is intended for vertical applications only and should never be used as decking. As with any fascia, you should always miter the ends at the corners for the best appearance (*see the opposite page for more on this*).

Installing Trim

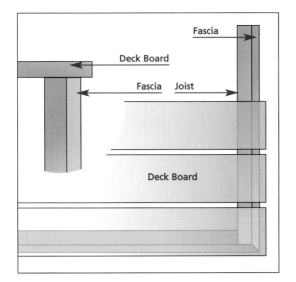

Overhanging deck boards If your deck boards are designed to extend past the rim joists and you want to cover them with a decorative piece of trim (the fascia), install the fascia *as shown in the drawing at left.* Basically, you butt the fascia boards up against the underside of the deck boards and miter them at the corners for best appearance. Typically the fascia is secured to the rim joists with galvanized nails or trim-head stainless-steel screws to minimize the visual impact of the fastener.

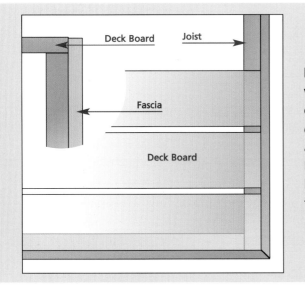

Flush deck boards If the deck boards were cut flush with the rim joists, you'll install the fascia so that the top edge is flush with the top of the deck boards (*see the drawing at left*). This type of trim is sometimes referred to as "picture frame" because the trim frames the decking. It's a good idea when installing fascia this way to leave a bit of a gap between the ends of the deck boards and the fascia for drainage and to allow for wood movement.

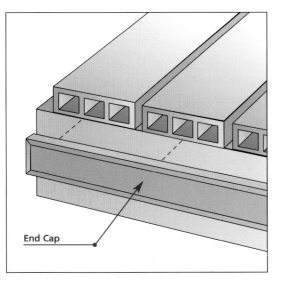

End caps If the deck boards you've installed are one of the new composites, especially one of the extruded varieties, you'll want to cover the exposed ends with either some type of fascia or the end caps supplied by the manufacturer of the composite decking. End caps are basically thin strips of the same material as the composite decking and are sized to conceal the ends. Some end caps have clips that snap into the ends of the boards; others are attached with small galvanized screws.

Chapter 5
Deck Accessories

Although by itself a deck is a fine thing, you can improve both its appearance and its function by adding a number of accessories. The most common accessory, and the one that provides the largest visual impact, is a deck railing. Whether the railing is simple or complex, it needs to be designed with safety in mind. Although most municipalities follow the Uniform Building Code (UBC) specifications for railing height, baluster spacing, and allowable clearances, some do not. It's imperative that you check with your local building inspector before starting on it to make sure your railing meets code.

In this chapter, I'll begin by going over the parts of a deck railing system and the typical ways that they're attached to decks, recommended code requirements, and options for balusters and lattice (*pages 69–71*). Then I'll show you a step at a time how to install the main structural support of a railing system—the deck posts (*pages 72–74*). I've included a simple-to-make drilling guide that will add accuracy to the job while greatly simplifying it.

Next, there are step-by-step instructions on how to add the deck rail that supports the balusters (*page 75*). Then on to the balusters (*pages 76–77*). To finish off the deck railing, I like to install a deck rail (deck cap) on top of the rails and posts to protect them and to add a decorative touch (*page 78*).

But railings aren't the only popular deck accessory. Built-in seating is one of the great add-ons that will let you relax and enjoy your new deck. I've included directions on how to install three different kinds of benches: a post-supported bench (*pages 79–80*), a railing-supported bench (*pages 81–82*), and a no-back bench (*pages 83–84*). Although many folks wouldn't think of fascia and skirting as deck accessories, they are: They're both optional items that you can add to a deck to dress it up. See *pages 85–87* for installing skirting and *page 88* for fascia.

Finally, there's a section on building stairs (*pages 89–92*)—everything from calculating rise and run to installing a concrete pad for a solid foundation. I've also included a section on building stairs with composite materials, as some of these materials require special care and installation (*page 93*).

Railing Post Options

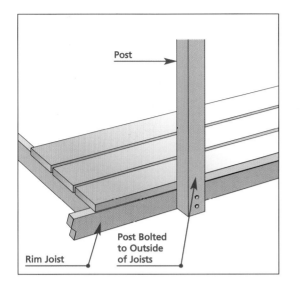

Post

Post Bolted
to Outside
of Joists

Rim Joist

Posts attach to outside of joists The simplest way to attach railing posts to a deck is to bolt them to the outside face of the rim joists; *see the drawing at left.* This method looks fine from the deck side but doesn't project the neatest appearance from the deck's exterior. There are, however, a couple of ways to camouflage the posts. One way is to cut notches on the bottom end so the post fits over the rim joists. Although this does create a slimmer profile, it also weakens the post. Another option is to miter the bottom end for a cleaner look (*see page 72*).

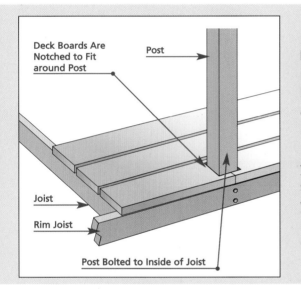

Deck Boards Are
Notched to Fit
around Post

Post

Joist

Rim Joist

Post Bolted to Inside of Joist

Posts attach to inside of joists A less conspicuous but more labor-intensive way to attach deck railing posts is to bolt them to the inside face of the rim joists; *see the drawing at left.* This method also takes advance planning because the posts need to be installed before the decking is laid down. The extra labor involved is twofold. First, you'll need to countersink the bolt holes in the rim joists so that the fascia will lie flat when it's installed. Second, you'll have to notch and fit the deck boards around the posts. On the plus side, this method provides the cleanest overall appearance.

COMMON RAILING TERMS

- **Balusters** – the vertical members of deck railing that divide up the space between the posts.

- **Cap rail** – a railing member that is laid flat horizontally across the tops of posts to provide a clean appearance, conceal the end grain of the posts, and keep out moisture.

- **Post** – a structural vertical member that is bolted to the rim joists and that supports the railing, balusters, and cap rails and post caps.

- **Post cap** – an optional accessory that fits on top of a post to give it a finished appearance.

- **Railing** – the horizontal members that span the distance between the railing posts and support all the balusters.

Continuous posts Another method for installing posts for a deck rail is to extend the posts that support the beam and connect to footings up high enough so that they can serve as a railing; *see the drawing at right.* Although this is one of the sturdiest ways to install a post, not only does it require the most advance planning, but also you may have to install additional posts (using one of the methods described on *page 69*) if the footings are spread too far apart to fully support the railing.

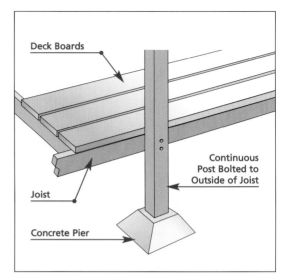

Deck Boards

Continuous Post Bolted to Outside of Joist

Joist

Concrete Pier

Code requirements for railings

Item Specified	Typical Requirement
Decks that require railings	All decks 30" or more in height
Stairways that require railings	All stairs with 5 or more steps
Height of railing	36" to 42"; usually 36" for residential and 42" for multi-use or commercial applications
Space between balusters	4" to 6" maximum
Space between balusters and posts	4" to 6" maximum
Space between bottom rail and deck	2" to 4" maximum

POST CAPS

One of the ways you can dress up a deck railing is to add caps to the posts. There is a wide variety of caps available, ranging from simple metal "roof"-style caps to complex metal and plastic caps that house low-voltage lighting (*see the photo at right*). Other varieties include "screw-on" caps; these typically have a turned profile with a ball on top. To install one of these, simply drill a hole in the end of the post, add a dollop of silicone caulk, and screw it in. New hybrid styles combine metal (usually copper) and wood to create a distinctive look.

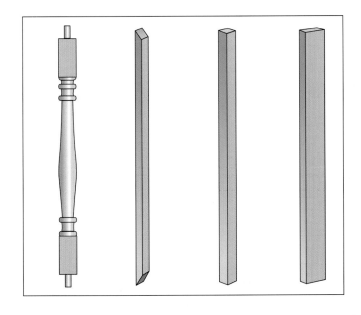

Baluster variations

The parts of a railing system that present the largest visual impact are the balusters. Since these provide the homeowner with the ability to create their own look, manufacturers offer a wide variety of both material choices and baluster profiles. The two most common material choices are pressure-treated lumber and cedar. In some areas of the country (particularly the West Coast), you'll also be able to find redwood balusters. Note that some of the composite decking manufacturers are beginning to make railing parts out of the same low-maintenance materials as their decking.

Profiles vary from simple squares to intricately turned spindles; *see the drawing at left.* Many manufacturers combine the two to create balusters that offer a nice profile but also provide flat surfaces for easy attachment to the railing or the fascia.

Lattice

Although most railing systems use balusters between the posts to create a barrier, another option is to install lattice. The only problem with using lattice is that it's nowhere near as strong as balusters. To create a safe and strong barrier using lattice, you'll need to support the lattice every 24" or so with vertical studs fastened to the railing. The best method I've found to hold the lattice in place is to cut grooves in the vertical supports and the railing to "capture" it; *see the drawing at left.*

For balusters that are attached directly to the fascia (*as shown in the drawing*) it's always a good idea to trim the bottom ends at an angle. This does a couple of things. First, it looks better. Second, it helps the baluster shed water by directing it to a point. And third, its trimmer profile is less likely to catch a piece of clothing or accidentally poke a child.

Installing Deck Posts

The critical parts of a deck railing system are the posts. That's because the posts support the entire system, including the railing, balusters, and end caps. Obviously, it's important that the posts be firmly attached to the deck, and spaced the appropriate distance apart to fully support the other parts. Consult your deck plans for the recommended placement, and don't forget to check with your local building inspector to make sure this spacing meets code requirements.

As I mentioned on *pages 69–70,* you can attach the posts to the rim joists a number of ways. For the deck *shown here,* I chose to bolt them to the exterior of the rim joists after the fascia was installed. I prefer this method because then I can run the balusters all the way down to the deck floor and fasten them to the fascia as well (*see pages 76–77*). The advantage to this is that infants and small pets can't possibly slip under the bottom rail—since there isn't one.

1 Measure and cut posts The first step to installing posts for a railing is to measure, mark, and cut the posts to length. If you're using manufactured posts, this may or may not be necessary. Also remember that a simple post (*like the one shown here*) is usually a lot cheaper to make yourself from standard 8' lengths of 4×4 than to purchase individually. If you're planning on softening the profile at the end of the post by mitering it, now is the time to do that as well.

2 Lay out holes In order to bolt the posts firmly to the rim joists, you'll need to drill holes near the bottom of each post for the bolts. Consult your deck plans, and then measure up from the bottom and mark the locations of a pair of holes. Use a speed square (*as shown*) or combination square to locate the exact center of the post. Space the bolt holes as far apart as possible while still leaving sufficient room for the countersinks that you'll drill in the next step.

3 **Drill countersink** Although not an absolute necessity, I recommend recessing the bolt heads in the posts to create a cleaner profile and to prevent them from catching on clothing, kids, or pets. Measure the diameter of the washers you'll be using with the bolts, and select a spade bit that's at least $\frac{1}{16}$" larger in diameter so you can insert the washer without having to force it. The idea here is to drill the holes to a consistent depth to leave the head of the bolt flush with the post once it's installed.

4 **Drill bolt holes** After you've drilled the countersinks, you can drill the actual holes for the bolts. Here again, you'll want to select a drill bit that's just slightly larger than the diameter of the bolt so that it will pass easily through the post. Since you'll be drilling through a minimum of $3\frac{1}{2}$" of wood, it's worth the investment to purchase a long bit. Just remember to stop periodically and back out the drill so you can clear the flutes of the bit to prevent clogs.

5 **Mark post locations on deck** At this point, the posts are ready to go; all that's left is to locate where they'll go on the deck, drill some pilot holes, and bolt them in place. Consult your deck plans and then measure and mark the location of the posts directly on the fascia (*see the photo at left*). Take the time to double-check these measurements—you don't want to be drilling errant holes in the fascia that you'll have to plug later.

6 **Drill holes in fascia** Although you can measure down and mark each hole location directly on the fascia, a more accurate way to do this is to use a simple drilling guide; *see the sidebar below.* To use the guide, place the T portion of the guide on the deck/fascia and slide it over until the centerline of the jig aligns with the mark you made on the deck. Then, holding it firmly in place, drill through each of the holes into the fascia. Remove the jig and drill deeper if necessary.

7 **Attach posts** Now you can attach the posts to the deck with bolts. Here again, it's best to secure the posts with through bolts and nuts instead of using the weaker lag bolts. As always, it's a good idea to give each bolt hole a shot of silicone caulk before installing the bolt to prevent water from traveling down the threads of the bolt. Tighten the two bolts friction-tight, and then use a level to make sure the post is plumb. When it is, give the bolts another one-half turn or so.

SIMPLE DRILLING GUIDE

The deck I installed here needed 14 posts for the railing. Whenever I'm faced with a repetitive task like locating and drilling the holes necessary for a job like this, I build a simple jig. A drilling jig like the one *shown here* not only adds accuracy to the job, it also makes it go a lot quicker. The drilling guide is just two scraps of 2×4 screwed together to form a T. Some careful measuring is all it takes to locate the holes to match the posts. Note: Use a bit sized to create pilot holes for the bolts in the jig—not the larger bit that you used to drill holes in the posts.

Installing Railing

1 **Cut parts** Once the posts are in place, you can turn your attention to the railing. The railing spans the posts and supports the balusters. How you attach the railing to the posts depends on the design of your railing. For railings that fit between the posts, you'll need a top and a bottom railing (*see page 77 for attachment options*). The railing system *shown here* requires only a top rail. Measure, mark, and cut the railing to size (*see the photo at left*).

2 **Attach to posts** Consult your deck plans to determine how they recommend you fasten the railing to the posts. For the railing *shown here,* it's simply screwed to each of the posts with a pair of 3" deck screws. Make sure before you secure both ends of the railing to check it with a level. Raise or lower the end of the railing as necessary to make it level, and fasten it to the post (*see the photo at left*).

3 **Scarf joint to join pieces** In many cases, you'll need to join pieces of railing together to form a continuous rail. Although you could simply butt the pieces together so that they meet at the post, a less-conspicuous method is to join them with a scarf joint. This is nothing more than cutting opposing 45-degree miters on the ends of the rail pieces so that the overlap occurs at the post. This way you can fasten both pieces to the post at the same time as you drive in screws; *see the photo at left.*

Installing Balusters

As with most deck railing parts, how the balusters attach to the railing will depend on the design of your system and the type of baluster you're using. The method of attachment *shown here* for balusters that attach to a top rail and then the deck/fascia is simple and easy to do. But this applies to most balusters. Installation is simple; it is just often tedious, as there are so many balusters. For balusters that fit between rails, the best method I've found for installing them is to build sections to fit between the posts "ladder-style." That is, cut the rails to length, then measure and mark the baluster locations. Next, screw a baluster at each location to one of the rails, position the top rail, and screw this to each of the balusters. Now, with the aid of a helper, lift the section and position it between the posts (fasten the rails to the posts using one of the methods shown in the sidebar on *page 77*).

1 **Cut the balusters** As with the posts, you can buy premade balusters or make your own. In either case, you'll likely need to cut them to length. Since the average deck will need anywhere from 75 to 100 balusters, it's best to measure and cut the balusters in batches. Another option is to set up a stop block on your power miter saw so you can butt the baluster up against it and then quickly cut it to length (*see the photo at right*).

2 **Mark hole locations** Since balusters are usually only 1½" thick, I like to drill shank holes for the screws I'll be using to fasten them to the deck and railing, to prevent them from splitting. For the best appearance, these holes should all line up, so I take the time to mark hole locations on the top and bottom of each baluster. Rather than doing this one at a time, group several together and mark all of them at once (*see the photo at right*).

3 **Drill pilot holes** Select a drill bit that's slightly larger in diameter than the shank of the screws you'll be using to attach the balusters. Then drill completely through the baluster at each marked hole location—typically two points at each end of the baluster. Here again, if you do this in batches, it'll go a lot quicker (*see the photo at left*).

4 **Attach to rails and fascia** Starting at one of the posts, space the first baluster the appropriate distance away and secure it to the railing and fascia with screws. I use a straight scrap of 2×4 as a spacer (with the face flat against the railing); I just insert it between the balusters, pull it tight, and screw the baluster in place. This provides for 3½" spacing, which is better than code (4" to 6" maximum allowed in most areas). Some might consider this overkill, but in my mind, safety comes first when it comes to railings.

RAIL ATTACHMENT OPTIONS

Wood Cleats: The simplest way to attach rails to posts is to screw a cleat to the post and then screw the rail to the cleat.

Cleat

Angle Iron: A sturdier version of the wood cleat, short lengths of angle iron serve the same purpose but will hold up better over time.

Angle Iron

Dado: A dado cut into the post forms a pocket to accept a rail. This method is strong but requires advance planning and some woodworking skills.

Dado

Installing a Cap Rail

① **Attach to posts** A cap rail, or deck cap, does a couple of things. It adds to the overall appearance of a railing system and, more importantly, shields the posts and balusters from rain. Although you can attach a deck cap by screwing through the cap directly into the posts or railing, I recommend attaching it from underneath. Angled metal brackets work well for this; *see the photo at right.* The advantage of doing it this way is there are no fasteners exposed on top to mar the appearance and collect water.

② **Plane to shed water** Most cap rails are flat. That's too bad, because flat surfaces tend to collect water. On way to prevent this from happening is to cut the posts (and balusters if necessary) at a slight angle (about 5 degrees) before installing the deck cap. This slight incline will help shed water. Another method I often use is to plane matching inclines on both sides of the cap rail to create sort of a "roof"; *see the photo at right.* The best tool for this job is a portable handheld planer; *see the sidebar below.*

PORTABLE PLANERS

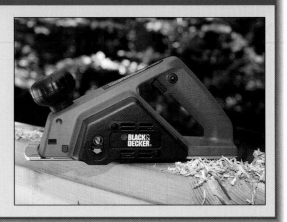

A portable power planer is basically a motorized hand plane. Most are capable of removing anywhere from 1/64" to 1/16" of wood in a single pass—without the elbow grease needed to operate a hand plane. Blade widths vary from 3" to almost 5", more than enough to handle most jobs. All feature an adjustable depth of cut, and most come with grooves in the base to make chamfering (trimming the edge of a board at a 45-degree angle) a snap. Cost ranges from around $40 up to $150; you can also pick one up for a day at most local rental centers for around $15.

Post-Supported Bench

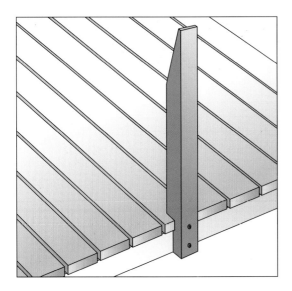

1 **Bolt posts to joist at hanger** You can substitute a post-supported bench like the one *shown here* for part of a railing system, or it can replace the railing entirely. Installing the bench posts is similar to installing posts for a railing (*see pages 72–74*) except that you'll want to cut a long taper on the inside top edges to create an angled backrest (you can skip this step for straight backs—they're just not as comfortable). You can make this cut by hand or with a reciprocating saw fitted with a long blade.

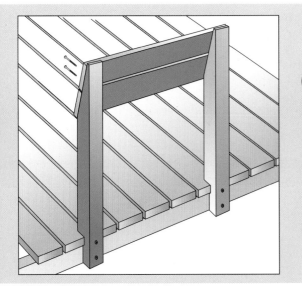

2 **Attach back supports** After you've bolted the bench posts securely to the deck, the next step is to add the back supports. In most cases, this will be two 2×6s (*see the drawing at left*). Measure, mark, and cut these 2×6s to span as far as possible between posts. Wherever back supports need to be joined together to create a longer length, use a scarf joint (*see page 75*). Screw each back support to a post, using galvanized screws. Make sure the supports are level before attaching them.

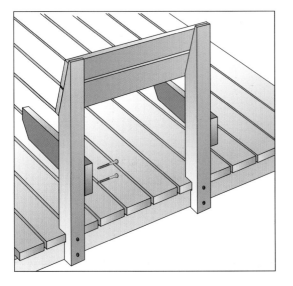

3 **Add seat supports** To create the seats, start by cutting one or two (depending on your design) seat supports for every post. Obviously, two supports per post will hold up better under heavier loads. As a general rule, you'll want the seat support to extend past the post the width of three or four 2×6s (about 16" for three). For optimum support, drill holes though the seat supports and posts and install bolts with washers and nuts. Alternatively, attach them with lag screws or deck screws.

4 **Add leg supports** To support the opposite end of the seat, add leg supports that run from the seat support to the deck. These can either be cut to fit under the seat support or be cut longer and attached to the sides of the seat supports with screws. In either case, you'll want to secure each leg support to the deck boards by driving in a couple of screws at an angle, as if your were toenailing.

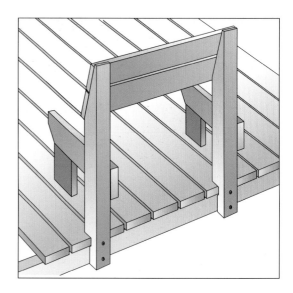

5 **Add seat planks** The last step is to add the seat planks. Here again, you'll want to measure, mark, and cut these as long as possible. Attach each plank to a seat support with a pair of 3" deck screws (*see the drawing at right*). When you're near the end of the plank, drill pilot holes to prevent splitting. Also, it's a good idea to knock off the sharp edges of the front planks. Do this with a roundover bit in a handheld router, with a power planer (*see page 78*), or by hand with a file or plane.

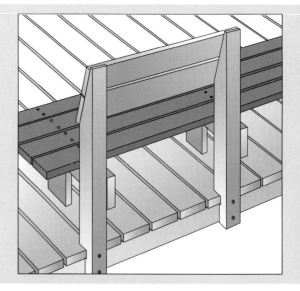

POST-SUPPORT OPTION

Another method of creating a built-in angled-back bench is to use angled 2×6s or 2×8s instead of posts (*see the drawing at right*). With this option, you'll need to install the back supports prior to attaching the deck boards. Since angling the back support like this creates a lever-type action when stressed, it's very important that the back support be bolted to the field joists and not screwed. Screws just don't have the holding power to handle the stresses involved with an angled support.

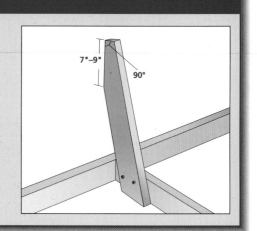

Railing-Supported Bench

1 **Cut parts** Here's a way to add a built-in bench to a deck that already has a railing. This is a good method for situations where you want to add only partial seating. The design *shown here* is based on a simple frame that's screwed together. Start by cutting the parts to length; experiment with the angles until you find the combination that feels the best. The seat should be long enough to support three 2×6s, and the back piece should fit under the end cap of your railing.

2 **Build the frame** After you've settled on a design and cut the parts to size, you can assemble the frames. Position the back post and front leg on the deck, and lay the seat support on top. Adjust the position of the pieces so the angled cuts line up. Screw the parts together at each connection with at least three 2½"-long deck screws. If you've got a lot of these to build, consider making a simple assembly jig to position the parts and hold them in place while you screw them together.

3 **Attach frame to the top rail** Once all the frames have been assembled, you can attach them to the railing. Start by measuring and marking their locations. Then set a frame in place so the bottom of the frame rests flat on the deck, and screw through the back support into the railing, *as shown in the photo at left.* Secure the back support with at least two screws spaced about 2" to 3" apart.

4 **Attach to deck** To attach the bottom of each frame to the deck boards, begin by butting a level up against the side of the frame and then adjust its position so it's plumb. Hold the frame firmly in place, and drive a couple of screws through the bottom of the frame at an angle and into the deck boards (*see the photo at right*). Whenever possible, do this over the joists and use screws that are long enough to penetrate into them.

5 **Cut and install seat planks** With the frames firmly attached to the deck boards and railing, you can add the seat planks. Measure, mark, and cut these planks as long as possible. Anytime you need to join planks together to make a longer board, use a scarf joint (*see page 75*) and position the joint directly over a seat frame. Secure the planks to the seat frames with 3" deck screws. As always, drill pilot holes near the ends to prevent splitting.

6 **Attach the back rest** All that's left to complete the bench is to add the back rest. In most cases, a pair of 2×6s will do the job. Start with the top board, *as shown in the photo*, and then add the lower board. Just as with the seat planks, you'll want to make the back rest boards as long as possible and use scarf joints whenever you need to join boards together.

No-Back Bench

One of the simplest built-in benches you can make is the no-back bench *shown here.* Although simple, it does require some advance planning—you'll need to attach the posts that support the bench to the field joists before installing the deck boards; *see Step 1 below.* Note that although I don't show the deck boards installed here, you would normally do this before proceeding with the bench construction.

Note also that the no-back bench isn't for everyone. It might be simple to build and install, but it's not the most comfortable way to sit. For maximum comfort, an angled back support is best (*see pages 79–82*). A no-back bench, however, does offer the advantage of providing an excellent spot for sunbathing—especially if you make the seat wider, using four 2×6s. This provides plenty of room to stretch out comfortably.

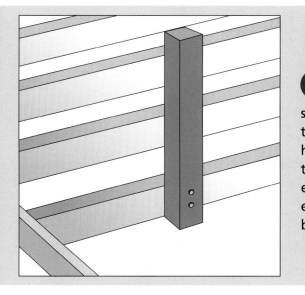

1 **Attach posts** The first step to installing the no-back bench is to attach the posts to the field joists that support the bench. Start by measuring, marking, and cutting to length all the posts you'll need. Next, drill shank holes in the posts and field joists for the bolts that secure the posts. Here again, through bolts with nuts and washers are much sturdier than lag screws. Don't forget to give each bolt hole a shot of silicone caulk before installing the bolts to help keep out moisture.

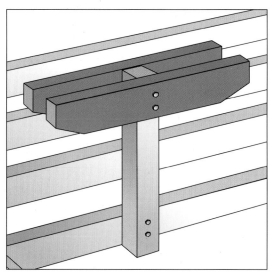

2 **Add seat supports** The next step is to cut and install the crosspieces that support the seat planks. The length of the seat supports will depend on whether you want to use three or four 2×6s. Whichever you decide, it's a good idea to cut tapers on the bottom edges—this improves the appearance and eliminates sharp corners. Make a pair of seat supports for each post, and drill holes through them and the post for through bolts, nuts, and washers. Alternatively, you can attach them with screws, but they'll be far weaker.

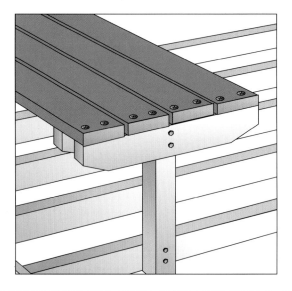

3 **Install seat planks** With the seat supports in place, you can install the seat planks. Start by measuring, marking, and cutting these to length. Use boards that are as long as possible; and if you need to join them together, use a scarf joint (*see page 75*) and position the joint over a seat support. Fasten each seat plank to the underlying support with a pair of 3" deck screws. Remember to drill pilot holes near the ends of the boards to prevent splitting.

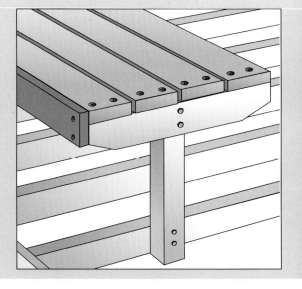

4 **Add side caps** The next two steps are optional, as they add little to the overall strength of the bench but do help with appearance. To conceal the end grain of the seat supports, consider adding side caps. These are nothing more than lengths of wood (either 2-by or 1-by) that are attached to the ends of the seat supports. Capping the sides like this not only covers the seat supports but also reduces the likelihood of catching clothing on them. Cut lengths as long as possible, and attach them to the supports with 3" or longer deck screws.

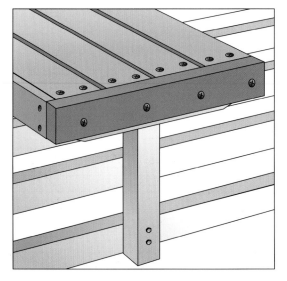

5 **Attach end caps** Another optional trim piece for the no-back bench is the end cap *shown in the drawing at right.* This short piece is added solely to conceal the end grain of the seat planks to give a more finished appearance. Cut the pieces to length and attach them to the seat planks and/or seat supports with galvanized screws or nails.

Installing Skirting

Railing adds a finishing touch to the top of a deck; skirting finishes off the bottom. Besides covering up the foundation and the footings, skirting also serves to limit access under the deck. This is particularly useful in keeping stray animals from selecting the space under your deck as their favorite fighting, mating, or birthing place. Finally, skirting helps block leaves and other wind-blown refuse from accumulating under the deck.

There are a number of materials options for skirting (or lattice, as it's often called): pressure-treated, cedar, redwood, and plastic. Although I really am a wood guy at heart, I recommend plastic skirting whenever possible. This stuff requires no finish whatsoever, it is virtually maintenance-free, and it will last a long, long time. Regardless of what type you use, I recommend fastening it with stainless steel screws since they are the least likely to cause staining.

1 **Measure space under deck** The first step to installing skirting or lattice under a deck is measuring the space. Use a tape measure to determine both the width and length of the space to be filled. Measure at both the top and bottom of the posts in case they're not even. Also, measure down to the ground at both posts and subtract an inch or so from this to prevent the lattice or skirting from touching the ground. The idea here is to get it close to the ground, but not touching. This discourages insects from traveling up the skirting and also helps reduce damage due to moisture.

2 **Assemble frame** After you've measured the space under the deck, you can cut 2×2 frame pieces to length (use pressure-treated lumber). For short spans (*like the one shown here*), you can usually get by with an upside-down U-shaped frame. For wider spans, you'll need to add a frame piece at the bottom, as well, to fully support the lattice. Screw the top frame piece to the beam and then screw the side frame pieces to the posts, *as shown.*

3 **Lay out lattice** Measure the height and width of the frame you've installed, and transfer this to a piece of lattice. I'm using white plastic lattice *here* since it's virtually impervious to weather. Lay out cut lines on the lattice with a chalk line, *as shown in the photo at right.* Note: Because the lattice is so flimsy, you'll want to lay it out on a piece of plywood supported by a pair of sawhorses.

4 **Cut lattice to fit frame** Now that you've laid out the lattice, you can cut it to size. The plastic lattice *shown here* can be easily cut with a standard circular saw or trim saw. You can also cut this stuff (or any lattice, for that matter) with a saber saw, reciprocating saw, or hand-saw. Keep in mind that the strips of wood lattice are often held together with staples, so it's best to use a demolition blade when cutting wood lattice.

5 **Provide proper clearance** After you've cut the lattice to size, check the fit by temporarily holding it up against the frame. Here's a good time to check for proper clearance—before you attach it to the frame. If you can slide your fingers under the base of the lattice *as shown here,* you've got it right. More than this, and vermin and other small beasties will soon discover how nice it is under the deck. Less than this, and you'll encourage water and insect damage.

6 **Drill pilot holes** Once you're happy with the fit of the lattice, you can install it. Because the small strips of the lattice (whether they're plastic or wood) can split easily, I always drill pilot holes. Select a bit that's slightly smaller than the diameter of the screws you're using, and drill pilot holes along the perimeter of the lattice every 12" or so (*see the photo at left*).

7 **Attach frame** Now you can attach the lattice to the frame. Hold the frame in place so that the top edge butts up against the beam and the lattice is centered from side to side. Then drive 1½" galvanized screws through the lattice and into the frame (*see the photo at left*). Fasten the top of the lattice first, starting in the center and working toward the ends, and then fasten the lattice to the side frame pieces.

A HINGED PANEL FOR EASY ACCESS

Since you'll likely need to eventually get under the deck for something (repairs, winterizing, hiding from the I.R.S., etc.), it's a good idea to add hinges to one of the lattice panels for easy access. Use galvanized or zinc-plated hinges, and attach them to the lattice with through bolts, nuts, and washers. Screw the hinges to the frame pieces, and attach the sides with a latch hook, like the kind you'd use to secure a screen door.

Installing Fascia

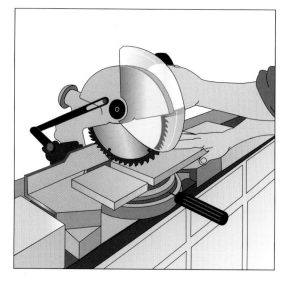

1 **Cut boards to length** Fascia is trim that you apply around the perimeter of a deck to cover the rim joists. In most cases, this will by 1-by material, usually a 1×10. Fascia can be installed flush with the deck boards or underneath them; *see page 67 for more on this.* The first step to installing fascia is to cut it to length. As usual, use the longest boards possible, as this cuts down on the number of joints. When you do need to join pieces together, use a scarf joint (*see page 75*).

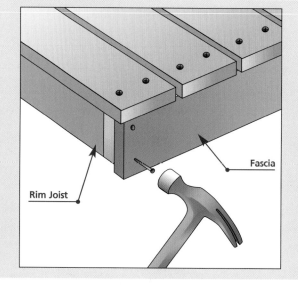

2 **Attach to rim joists** There are a number of ways to attach fascia to the rim joists using either screws or nails. The cleanest method is also the most work; it involves screwing it to the rim joist from behind. The next cleanest method is to attach it with galvanized casing nails or finish nails (although this is the least secure method). If you choose instead to attach the fascia from the front with screws, consider using stainless-steel trim-head screws to minimize the visual impact of the screws.

Rim Joist

Fascia

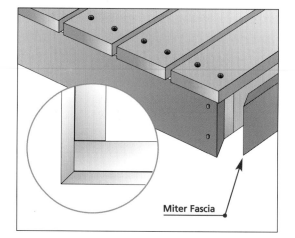

3 **Miter corners for clean look** For the cleanest possible appearance, you should always join the fascia at the corners with miters (*see the drawing at right*). Your best bet for cutting an accurate miter (a bevel, technically) on the end of a wide board is to use a cutting jig to guide a circular saw. (*For more on building a shop-made cutting guide, see page 47.*) If you notice any gaps after the fascia is installed, you can "burnish" the miter closed by rubbing the round shank of a screwdriver over the ends of the miter joint.

Miter Fascia

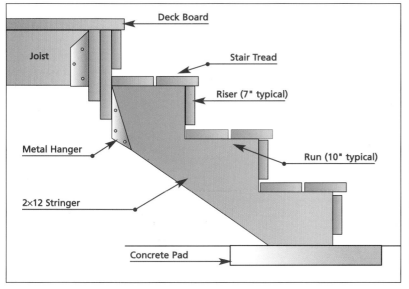

Labels on diagram:
- Deck Board
- Joist
- Stair Tread
- Riser (7" typical)
- Metal Hanger
- Run (10" typical)
- 2×12 Stringer
- Concrete Pad

Installing Steps

of the stairs will also by influenced by the materials used to construct it. The stairs *shown here* are made from pressure-treated wood. If your deck boards are made from composites, you should also be able to use them as treads, but note that these products should not be used to make the stringers.

Any deck that isn't a ground-level deck will most likely need steps. Although you can purchase pre-made steps, odds are that they weren't designed for your deck. Installing stairs requires a bit of number crunching and some additional concrete work (*see the sidebar on page 91*). If neither of these sounds like much fun, consider contracting out this portion of the job. Note that the design

A typical set of deck stairs is shown in the drawing *above left.* They consist of two or three stringers (the foundation of the stairs), stair treads, and vertical risers, which close off the spaces between the treads. The stringer attaches to the deck via metal joist hangers and is fastened at the bottom to a concrete pad.

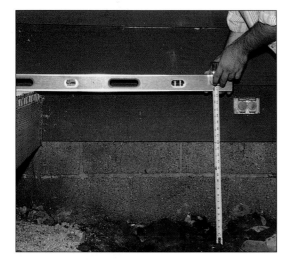

1 **Establish rise and run** All of the math involved in building stairs has to do with making the stringers. The first step (pardon the pun) is to establish the rise and run of the steps. The total rise is determined by measuring from the ground to the top of the deck boards at the lowest spot. The easiest way to do this is to extend a level out past the deck and measure down from there; *see the photo at left.*

Divide this measurement by 7" (the recommended unit rise) to determine the number of steps (round off to the nearest whole number). Now divide your measured total rise by the number of steps to determine your actual unit rise. The step run is easy to determine. If you're planning on using two 2×6s, your unit run is 10"—this allows for a gap between them plus a slight overhang. Finally, you can calculate the total span (how far out the stairs will go) by multiplying the unit run by the number of treads (always one less than the number of steps).

2 **Lay out the stringers** With unit rise and unit run calculated, you can lay out the stringers. Mark the unit rise on the short leg of a framing square, and mark the unit run on the other leg. Start at the top of the stringer and place the square so that the marks align with the edge of the stringer, *as shown.* Trace the outline of the square on the stringer with a pencil. When you get to the bottom step, shorten the rise by the thickness of the tread material. Then go back and lay out a line 1½" below each tread (the thickness of the tread material).

3 **Cut the steps** Now that the stringers have been laid out, you can cut out the notches for the treads. The best tool for the job here is a circular saw. As you make the cuts, make sure to stop ½" or so before you reach the inside corners. Once all the cuts have been made, go back and finish the cuts with a handsaw and remove the waste. Whenever possible, use a speed square as a guide to ensure a straight cut.

4 **Attach brackets** Although there are a number of ways to attach the stringers to the deck, I prefer to use metal angle brackets, like those *shown in the photo at right.* Start by attaching one bracket to the inside top edge and the inside bottom edge of the two outside stringers. Then install brackets to both sides of the top and bottom of the middle bracket. Use galvanized joist hanger nails for maximum shear strength.

A CONCRETE PAD

One of the most common mistakes most folks make when they add a set of stairs to a deck is to skip the concrete pad under the stringers. Quite often they'll just pour some gravel or sand there and hope that it does the job. It won't. A concrete pad does several things for you. First, it creates a solid footing for the stringers—one that won't sink over time. Second, it lifts the stringers up off the ground to help keep them dry and less susceptible to damage from insects. Third, a concrete pad provides the means to securely fasten the bottom of the stringers so they won't move or twist over time.

All in all, a pretty fair trade-off for not a whole lot of effort.

Installing a concrete pad is fairly straightforward. Basically, you level the ground, build a simple form from 2-by lumber, and mix and pour in the concrete (*see steps 1 and 2 below*). Check you local code to find out requirements for depth of concrete and whether reinforcing bar ("rebar") is required.

1 **Build and level form** Start by leveling the ground if necessary. Then build a form from 2-by lumber by screwing the ends together. Position the form at the desired location and check it for level. To improve drainage, it's a good idea to have the form angle slightly away from the deck and foundation of the house. Once it's in place, pound a couple of stakes into the ground next to the form, and screw the stakes to the form to keep it from shifting as you pour the concrete.

2 **Pour concrete** As an aid for drainage, I suggest adding a 1" to 2" layer of gravel to the bottom of the form. Mix up a batch of concrete according the manufacturer's directions, and pour it into the form. Continue mixing and pouring until the form is full, just slightly past the top. Let the concrete settle for about 15 to 20 minutes, and then screed the top level with a scrap of 2×4; *see pages 42–43 for more on working with concrete.*

5 Attach stringers to deck Locate and mark the locations of the three stringers on the deck directly on the fascia. Note that on some decks, it may be necessary to first install a support cleat under the fascia to provide a fastening spot for the brackets (*as shown here*). Position the stringer so that the bottom sits level on the concrete pad, and then attach the brackets on the stringers to the fascia with galvanized or stainless steel screws. Use every hole available in the bracket, for maximum support.

6 Attach stringers to pad Next, use a framing square to make sure the stringer is perpendicular to the fascia, and make a set of marks through the metal brackets onto the concrete pads to indicate where you'll drill holes. Drill these holes with a hammer drill that's fitted with a carbide-tipped masonry bit. I prefer to use Tap-cons (concrete screws) to fasten the brackets to the pad. A nut driver mounted in a driver/drill makes quick work of driving in the screws.

7 Attach treads All that's left is to add the treads. Cut these to length so that there's a 1" overhang past the stringers. Secure them to the stringers with 3" deck screws. Remember to first drill pilot holes near the ends of the treads before driving in screws, to prevent splitting. It's also a good idea to treat the cut ends of the treads with a preservative.

COMPOSITE STEPS

1 **Attach riser** Solid composite decking (such as Trex) can be installed just like wood treads. Extruded structural composite decking (like the TimberTech *shown here*) goes down a little different. First, the unit run is 11", and maximum stringer spacing is 16". Second, this system uses risers made from their fascia boards, and you start from the bottom up. Begin by cutting a riser that's 1⅛" higher than the bottom step. Then fasten it to the stringers with 2½" stainless steel screws, *as shown.*

2 **Fasten tread to riser** Once the first riser is in place, cut the tongue off the front stair tread only, using a circular saw and an edge guide or using a table saw (see the manufacturer's instructions for more on this). Then hook the tread over the riser that you just installed, and nail or screw it directly through the lip of the tread into the riser, *as shown.* Next attach the back edge of the tread to the stringers by screwing through the back edge at an angle, just as would if you were installing the plank as decking (*see page 65 for more on this*).

3 **Screw tread to stringer** Place the next plank directly behind the first, and engage the tongue in the groove. Use hand pressure only for this; do not try and force the parts together (there may be up to a ¼" gap between the planks). Then fasten the back edge of the plank to the stringers as you would for decking. To create the next step, place the next riser board directly on top of the plank you just installed, and repeat steps 1 and 2 for the remaining treads and risers.

Chapter 6

Porches and Overheads

There's nothing quite like enjoying a cool breeze on a hot summer day under the shade of a porch or overhead. Or watching a rain shower from the protection of a roofed porch. This is especially true if the porch or overhead is screened in to keep out pesky insects. It's no wonder, then, that many homeowners want to add a porch or overhang to an existing structure, or screen in an existing porch.

In this chapter, I'll start by going over the options you'll have for overheads. Consider what works best for you—a freestanding overhead or one that's attached to the house (*opposite page*). Next, I'll take you through one step at a time how to add an overhead screen to a deck, including a number of fill options to screen out the sunlight (*pages 96–97*).

Next, since many folks have a porch but wish it were screened in, I'll show you just how easy it is to make this dream a reality. It all starts with building a simple frame to hold the screens (*pages 98–100*). The frame is nothing more than pressure-treated 2×4s that are attached to your existing porch floor, walls, and ceiling. With a frame in place, adding the screening is a breeze. I'll show you how to install screening in one afternoon, using a nifty new product called

ScreenTight—everything from installing the base molding and rolling in the screen to covering this all up with a decorative cap (*pages 101–102*). Since no screened-in porch is complete without a screen door, I'll show you how to install one of these (*page 103*).

If you've been thinking about tearing up that old rotting porch floor or foundation, I'll show you how to do this, starting with ways to shore up the roof so that you can lift up the columns to access the flooring (*page 104*). Then on to ripping out and rebuilding the old foundation (*pages 105–107*), followed by step-by-step instructions on how to install the new flooring, including recommendations for flooring and finishes (*pages 108–109*).

Overhead Design Considerations

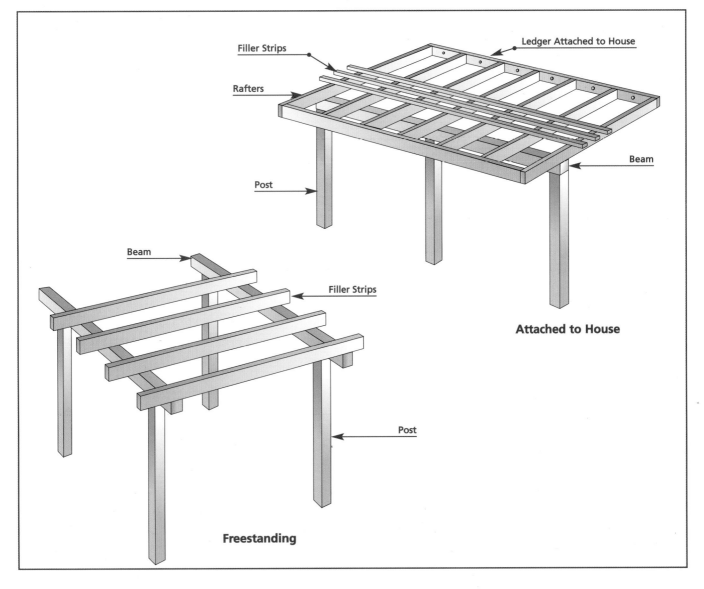

Filler Strips

Ledger Attached to House

Rafters

Beam

Post

Attached to House

Beam

Filler Strips

Post

Freestanding

The are two basic structural choices when you're adding an overhead to a deck or porch: The unit can be freestanding, or attached to the house. Since a freestanding structure like the one *shown above left* must support all of the weight of the unit, it usually consists of large beams, often with crossbraces to prevent racking.

Units that are attached to the house (like the one *shown above right*) require only one-half

the support structure because one-half of the weight is borne by the house. Freestanding overheads are most often screens (*see pages 96–97*) and, although they do offer some shade, are mainly decorative. Depending on the region, attached overheads may or may not be covered with shingles and angled to shed water. In areas that receive a lot of snow, any overhead needs to be designed and installed by a professional.

Building a Screen

1 **Attach posts to deck** The first step in building a deck screen is to locate the posts that will support the screen. The best method for attaching posts to deck boards is to use adjustable post base caps, like the one *shown here.* This type of framing connector raises the post off the deck and allows water to drain, reducing the risk of rot. For the most secure hold, bolt the post caps to the deck boards. Then insert a post in each cap, make sure it's plumb, and fasten it to the cap with galvanized nails.

2 **Install post caps** The next step is to attach post caps to the tops of the posts to accept the beams that span between them. These just slip over the ends and are secured with galvanized nails or screws. Note: Before you slip the cap on, it's a good idea to brush a coat of preservative onto the top of the post. Flat surfaces like this, even when covered, tend to collect moisture and are prone to rot and insect damage.

3 **Add the beams** Measure, mark, and cut the beams to length to span the posts. You can install the beams flush with the tops of the posts (*as shown here*) or allow them to overhang a bit for added visual interest. Have a helper assist in lifting each beam into place and have him or her hold the beam steady until you can secure it. Here again, either galvanized nails or screws will do.

4 **Attach bracing** To prevent racking, you should install braces between the posts and the beams. These can be simply lengths of 4×4 mitered at a 45-degree angle at each end. Secure the braces with galvanized deck screws or, better yet, with galvanized lag bolts for a stronger hold. Make sure to check that the post is perpendicular to the beam, using a framing square, before you attach both ends of the brace.

5 **Add the screen fill** At this point, you can add the screen fill to the top of the beams. There are many choices for fill (*see the sidebar below*), and how you install it will depend on the type. If you're using individual boards (*as shown here*), start at one end and screw the board to the beam. Then use a scrap-wood spacer to align the next board and fasten it in place. Repeat until the beam is covered. Since lattice is pre-assembled, it goes on a lot quicker—just make sure to support it periodically with cross supports to prevent it from bowing.

SCREEN FILL OPTIONS

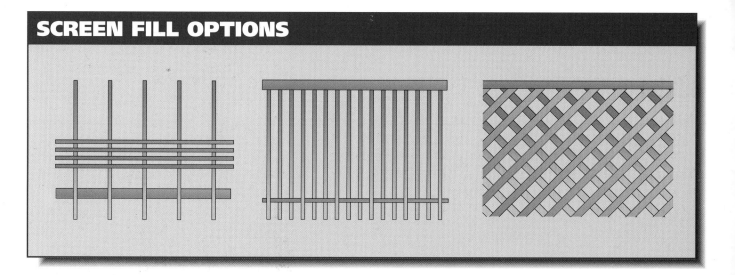

Screened Porch: Framing

A screened-in porch is one of life's simple pleasures. Although many folks think of one only as a way to keep out insects, a screened porch also offers another level of privacy—sort of an invisible shield that says "this is not a public space—it's one of the rooms of our house." The screens also keep leaves and other windswept debris from gathering on your porch floor. Combine all of these, and it's no wonder many homeowners would like to screen in their porch. In years past, this meant building and assembling individual screens. But a recent new product called ScreenTight has made screening in a porch not only an afternoon job, but also affordable as well; *for more on this, see page 101.* In order to install any screen system, you'll need to first build a simple frame to support the screening. This can be from floor to ceiling (*see the drawing below*) or from railing to ceiling, depending on the design of your porch. You'll also need to add a screen door; *see page 103 for directions on how to do this.*

1 **Cut frame pieces** If you're building a frame for the ScreenTight screening system, you'll need to keep openings to a maximum of 35 square feet—that's an amazing 5' × 7' expanse. The simplest framework consists of pressure-treated 2×4 sole plates, top plates, studs, and horizontal supports (*see the sidebar below*). Measure each space carefully and cut the pieces to length. I'd suggest cutting and installing the sole and top plates first and then cutting the studs to fit.

TYPICAL SCREEN FRAMING

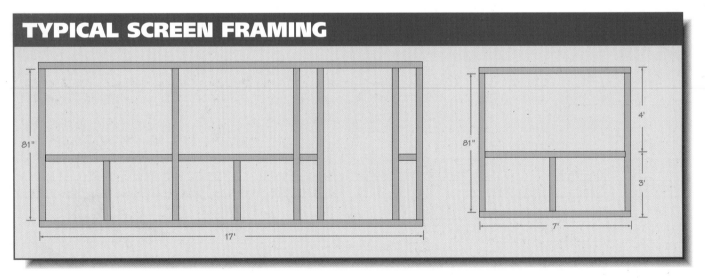

81"

17'

81"

4'

3'

7'

2 **Drill shank holes for fasteners** How you attach the sole plate to your porch floor will depend on what it's made of. For a wood floor, you can basically screw the pieces directly to it. For a masonry floor (like the one *shown here*), more steps are involved. The first thing to do is to drill shank holes for fasteners. I use special masonry screws called Tap-cons for this (*see the inset on page 100*). Select a drill bit that's slightly larger than the diameter of the screws, and drill shank holes every 24" in the sole plate.

3 **Transfer marks to floor** To transfer the shank hole locations to the masonry, place the sole plate in position on the floor and drill through each shank hole with a hammer drill fitted with a carbide-tipped masonry bit. If you're using Tap-cons, you'll be able to purchase the recommended bit at the same store where you purchased the screws. Drill just far enough to mark the location.

4 **Drill holes for fasteners** Now that you've marked each screw location, remove the sole plate and finish drilling the holes with the hammer drill and masonry bit. Note: You're always better off drilling too deep rather than not deep enough when using Tap-cons. A piece of tape wrapped around the drill bit will serve as a simple but effective depth stop. Make sure to blow out the dust from the hole when you're done drilling.

5 **Attach with tap-cons** Reposition the sole plate and thread a masonry screw into each shank hole. Whenever possible, I always use the type that has a hex head (*inset*) versus a slotted or Phillips head, as those tend to strip easily. With a hexhead screw you can use a nut driver or, better yet, a socket wrench to apply the required torque to drive the screw home. Be careful as the screwhead contacts the wood not to force it—a socket wrench can easily snap the screw.

6 **Attach top plates** With the sole plates installed, you can turn your attention to the top plates. In most cases, you can simply screw them into the ceiling or fascia (*as shown here*). Make sure to use galvanized screws and drive them in every 24" or so. Also, take the time to ensure that they're aligned with and parallel to the sole plate before fastening them in place—a plumb bob works best for this.

7 **Attach studs** Finally, measure, mark, and cut studs to fit between the sole plate and top plate. Attach them to the side walls whenever possible, and toenail them to the top and sole plate with nails or screws (*as shown here*). If your design calls for horizontal supports and braces (*see the drawing on page 98*), cut and install them now. Make sure to use a level when installing all parts so that they're level and plumb.

Screened Porch: Screening

1 **Apply molding** Once you've installed the frame, you can add the screening. To do this, start by installing the ScreenTight base molding to cover the frame. Measure and cut the base to fit. You can cut it with metal snips, a hacksaw, or a power miter box. One of the many beauties of this system is that there's no need to cut miters at the corners—just butt the strips together. Fasten the molding to the frame with 1" screws by driving one in every open slot and no less than 2" in from each end.

2 **Spline at top and sides** After you've installed all the base molding, you can install the screen. Use a quality fiberglass screening, and cut each piece roughly 6" wider and longer than needed. The best thing I've found to hold the screening in place so you can add the splines that lock it into the base is a push pin—just poke one through each corner of the screening and press it into the frame. Then you can install the spline (make sure to use 0.175"-diameter spline), starting with the top and then moving to the sides. Roll it into the grooves in the base molding, using a splining tool *as shown*.

THE SCREENTIGHT SYSTEM

ScreenTight is a nifty product that allows you to screen in a porch in an afternoon. It was developed and patented by a remodeling contractor who was convinced that there had to be a better way to screen in porches. Unlike conventional screening that relies on staples to secure the screen and trim to cover the staples, ScreenTight uses a rubber spline to lock the

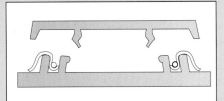

screen into a patented base molding (*see drawing above*), which is covered with an external cap. This cap (available in colors) snaps onto the base and further tightens the screen.

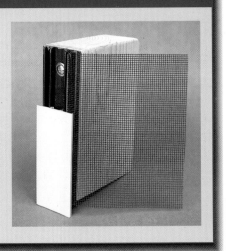

3 **Spline at bottom** After you've rolled the spline into the top and side, you can secure it to the bottom base molding. Although you don't need to pull the screening to tighten it, I've found that keeping it taut while rolling helps prevent kinks in the screening. Moderate pressure is all it takes to install the screening and spline, and this part of the job goes surprisingly fast. If for some reason there's a sag or kink in the screening, just pull the spline out, hold the screening taut, and reroll it.

4 **Remove excess screening** Now that the screening is locked in place, you can trim away the excess. You can use a pair of scissors or a sharp utility knife for this, but I recommend using ScreenTight's Roller Knife. It's a combination tool that not only rolls in spline, but also has a knife blade at one end that extends so you can neatly trim the excess off. What's nice about this is that you can use the roller wheel to "track" the cut along the spline to trim the screening evenly and consistently (*see the photo at right*).

5 **Apply decorative cap** Once you've installed all the screening and have trimmed off the excess, you can install the decorative cap. Measure, mark, and cut each piece to fit (just butt the ends together), and install the cap by tapping it firmly with a rubber mallet or a scrap of wood and a hammer. Start at one end and work toward the other. On vertical pieces, the cap will often slide down as you install it. Just grip it and push up to reposition the end and continue.

A Screen Door

1 **Frame opening** To install a screen door on a porch, the first thing you'll need to do is frame an opening for the door. Since the porch roof is fully supported by its columns, you don't have to worry about installing a header. Just measure the door and add an inch or so for clearance, and frame a rough opening like the one shown for the installed ScreenTight door *at left.* Whenever possible, attach the framework to a nearby wall and add horizontal supports between studs to add rigidity. Install the frame just as you did for the screening; *see pages 98–100.*

2 **Add hinges** The next step to installing a screen door is to add hinges. You can use standard door hinges (*as shown here*), or self-closing hinges that automatically close the door after it's been opened. I recommend installing three hinges spaced evenly along the side of the door, as this supports the door better. Attach the hinges to the door with galvanized wood screws, and then insert the door in the rough opening. Use shims to lift the door off the ground so it will swing freely. Then attach the loose hinge flaps to the frame and check for proper operation.

3 **Add door stops** Once the door is in place, you can add door stops to the frame. The door stops do two things. First, they prevent the door from swinging too far when it's closed. And second, they cover any gaps between the door and the frame that would allow in insects. Door stop is available at home centers in 8' to 16' lengths. Measure, mark, and cut each piece to length. Close the screen door and butt the stop up against it *as shown.* Then fasten it to the frame with galvanized nails. Paint the stop and frame to match the house trim.

Shoring Up a Roof

The thought of removing the supports for a porch roof will make most homeowners nervous—and it should. If not done properly, the whole thing could come crashing down. But that only happens when the roof isn't shored up correctly. This is not a complex task; it just requires the right equipment and the proper materials. If you need to remove the columns, I suggest using a combination of the two methods *shown*. First, use jacks to lift the roof up just enough to remove the columns or free them from the flooring. If you need to remove the flooring, you'll need to shore up the roof with braces so that you can remove the jacks.

Jacks

There are a number of jacks, either telescoping or hydraulic, that can be used to support or shore up a roof. Telescoping jacks are available at most rental centers and, once extended and locked in place with pins, can be used to support or raise the roof by turning a height-adjustment screw with a wrench or pin (*see the drawing above right*). Hydraulic jacks are available at most automotive stores and home centers and can be used to raise and lower a roof via a 4×4 beam. Whichever you use, make sure to protect both the porch floor and ceiling by inserting scraps between the jack pads and the finished surfaces.

Wood brace

A wood brace like the one *shown at right* is an economical way to support a porch roof so you can work on the columns, floor, or foundation. Since it has to bear a considerable weight, use a 2×10 or, better, a 2×12. Protect the edge of the porch roof or fascia with a scrap block *as shown*. For the best grip, cut a notch in the end of the brace to fit over the scrap block. Angle the brace no more than 60 degrees; secure the end on the ground to a stake that's set firmly into the ground.

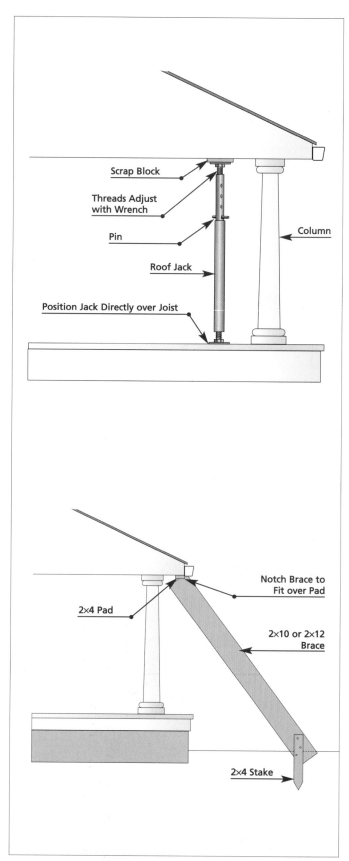

Scrap Block

Threads Adjust with Wrench

Pin

Roof Jack

Column

Position Jack Directly over Joist

2×4 Pad

Notch Brace to Fit over Pad

2×10 or 2×12 Brace

2×4 Stake

A New Porch Foundation

Wooden porch floors require periodic attention. You should expect to refinish a wood floor every three to five years, depending on weather conditions and direct exposure to sunlight. That's because a horizontal surface like a porch floor not only has to stand up to the elements, but also is constantly battered with use. In order to stand up to this constant use and abuse, the floor must be sealed properly to shed water and prevent rot and decay. When neglected, the flooring will quickly degrade and need to be replaced; *see pages 108–109 for more on this.* If the neglect is severe, the foundation is at risk, too. Fortunately, replacing either of these isn't difficult. The only complication is that the roof will need to be shored up because you'll have to lift the support columns off the flooring in order to replace it. If you are replacing a foundation, make sure to inspect the piers or footings that it rests on and make any repairs as needed (*see page 125 for more on repairing brick piers*).

1 **Shore up the roof** The first step to replacing a foundation is to shore up the roof so that you can lift the columns up off the flooring. Here again, I'd suggest using jacks to lift up the roof and braces to support the roof so that you can remove the jacks (*see the opposite page for more on shoring up a roof*). Attach the braces or posts securely to the roof or fascia with screws, *as shown here.* Inspect the footings of the columns to see how they're attached to the flooring, and remove any fasteners before lifting them off the flooring.

2 **Remove flooring** Once you've lifted the support columns off the flooring and have added braces and removed the jacks, you can rip out the old flooring. Wear leather gloves and eye protection, and use a crowbar or pry bar to persuade stubborn boards. In most cases, you'll be removing tongue-and-groove flooring. Pry up one end and you should be able to lift and pull the piece off. Pound over any exposed nails to prevent an accident.

3 **Remove rim joists** To remove the foundation, start by prying off the perimeter or rim joists. A sledgehammer makes this work go quickly if the foundation is nailed together. If it was screwed together, first try to back out the old screws before resorting to force. Be particularly careful as you remove the rim joists that connect to the ledger so that you don't weaken its connection—unless you're planning on replacing it as well (if this is the case, *see pages 52–54*). If the ledger is in good shape, check to make sure it's fastened securely to the house, and tighten or replace fasteners as needed.

4 **Remove field joists** Once the rim joists have been removed, you can take out the field joists. Depending on how your foundation was built, these may run parallel to the ledger. If this is the case, you'll have to remove one rim joist (*see Step 3 above*) and then lift and twist the field joist to free it from the opposite rim joist (*see the photo at right*). Then after you've removed all the field joists, you can remove the final rim joist.

5 **Install new rim joists** To build the new foundation, start by cutting the rim joists to length. Then place the two perpendicular rim joists on the piers and attach them to the ledger with 3" deck screws or lag bolts. Next, attach the rim joist that runs parallel to the ledger to the two you just installed (*see the photo at right*). If possible, use the old joists as templates to measure and cut the new rim joists.

6 **Check for square** Once the rim joists are in place, the next step is to check to make sure the frame is square. The best method I've found for this is to use a 3-4-5 triangle; *see page 37 for more on this.* Check the frame and adjust its position on the piers as necessary to square it up. Once it's square, nail or screw a temporary brace from one joist to another to keep it square until the flooring is installed.

7 **Install corner braces** I always recommend installing metal corner braces to wood foundations to add strength and rigidity to the frame. Make sure to purchase braces that are the full length of your 2-by material. Also, don't forget to use the recommended fastener—typically, galvanized joist hanger nails—and fill every hole available in the brace with nails.

8 **Attach new field joists** Finally, measure, mark, and cut field joists to fit between the rim joists— these will likely all run parallel to the ledger and house. You can use joist hangers (*as shown here*) to secure the field joists to the rim joists and simply screw them together. I prefer joist hangers because they more fully support the field joists and hold them in position better over time (*for more on installing joist hangers, see page 60*).

New Porch Flooring

1 **Acclimatize** Whether you're replacing old flooring or installing new flooring on a rebuilt foundation (*see pages 106–107*), you'll want to use pressure-treated tongue-and-groove flooring. To prevent problems due to the naturally occurring movement in wood, it's best to allow your new flooring to acclimatize to its surroundings before installation—typically one to two weeks. Keep the flooring off the ground, and protect it by loosely covering it with 4-mil plastic.

2 **Put first strip flush on end** To install tongue-and-groove flooring, start by fastening the first strip flush on one end so it's perpendicular to the house. To secure the first strip, you'll need to face-nail this piece to the rim joist and then blind-nail it to every joist *as shown in the photo at right.* Make sure to use galvanized nails—8d hot-dipped galvanized ring-shank nails are recommended. Also, it's important to leave at least ½" of clearance between the end of the strip and the house for expansion.

3 **Apply primer to edges** Here's a trick that the pros use to ensure a watertight seal. They brush on a coat of oil-based primer to both the tongue and the groove of mating boards before they install them (*see the photo at right*). This way the primer can form a seal within the joint. Although this takes a bit of effort, and will certainly slow down the installation, it's well worth the effort. Note: If you have a helper do this as you install the strips, it goes a lot faster.

④ Blind-nail second strip Once the starter strip is in place, you can begin installing the remaining strips of flooring (*see the photo at left*). For strips that don't snug up tightly against the previous piece, use one of the techniques *shown on page 48* to persuade the piece to fit. Don't worry about trimming the pieces to exact length; instead allow them to "run wild" so they extend out over the edge.

⑤ Trim flooring to length After all the flooring is installed, snap a chalk line on the flooring at the desired overhang (usually 1"). Then use a circular saw to trim all the boards to length at the same time (*see the photo at left*). Next, I like to rout a ⅜" roundover or chamfer on the front top edge to soften it and to help prevent the splintering that's bound to occur over time.

⑥ Apply a finish Finally, you can apply a finish to your new floor. The Southern Pine Council recommends that you begin with a coat of paintable water-repellent sealer on all four sides and the ends. After it has dried the recommended time, followed this by a coat of high-quality mildew-resistant oil-based primer for exterior use. A topcoat of oil-based porch enamel in the color of your choice is the finishing touch.

Chapter 7

Repair and Maintenance

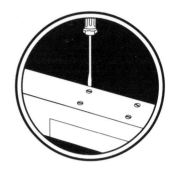

By their very nature, all decks and porches require routine maintenance and repair. Buffeted by the elements and under a constant barrage of foot traffic, tricycles, and pets, it's no wonder these need constant attention.

That's not to say that you need to jump up and run out to sweep off every leaf that lands on your deck, but it is important to keep these surfaces clean and well maintained. Your deck or porch, after all, is a very visible part of your home and in many cases a sizable investment. It's well worth the time and energy to keep it in tip-top condition.

I'll start this chapter by describing the various cleaners and finishes that you can use to maintain your deck (*opposite page*). Next, I'll take you through a suggested routine for cleaning your deck or porch (*pages 112–113*) and then show you how to apply a new finish or renew an old one (*pages 114–115*).

Then on to some repair work. Starting on *page 116,* I'll show you how to repair loose or damaged deck boards, followed by instructions on replacing a baluster (*page 117*). Next, there's advice on replacing a rail post (*page 118*) and installing a new stair tread (*page 119*). How to

repair a post and how to replace damaged or rotted skirting are shown on *pages 120 and 121, respectively.* If your porch floor needs work but replacing the entire floor isn't warranted (see *pages 105–109*), there's information on how to remove and replace just a small section or strip (*page 122*).

Likewise if you have a damaged porch column where the damage isn't structural and you don't need to replace the entire thing, I'll show you how you can make a repair with a nifty product called WoodEpox (*pages 123–124*). Finally, if any of your brick piers that support your porch are damaged, I'll show you how to make a repair without rebuilding the entire pier (*page 125*).

DECK CLEANERS AND FINISHES

Cleaners There are a number of chemical products available (often referred to as deck cleaners, brighteners, or deck wash) that can make quick work of renewing tired-looking deck boards; *see the photo at left.* All of these products typically contain a mild acid, either sodium hypoclorite or oxalic acid, that dissolves dirt and grime and chemically lightens the wood. Most can be sprayed on and will do their work without scrubbing—simply hose down the deck after waiting 10 to 15 minutes, and the deck is good as new.

Finishes When it comes time to protect the surface of a deck, you're faced with two basic choices: You can apply a water sealer (*see below*) or apply one of the many types of finishes (*see the photo at right*). The type of finish you choose will depend on how much wood grain you want to see and what kind of protection you're after. To see the most grain, use a clear wood finish. Select one with UV blockers to protect the wood from the sun. For less visible grain, choose a semitransparent stain. To hide the grain, use a solid-color stain.

Water Sealers The most popular finish used to protect a deck is a transparent water sealer (*see the photo at left*). Water sealers are penetrating-oil formulas that soak down into porous materials and create a moisture barrier that still allows the wood to breathe. Most sealers dry clear and allow the wood to weather naturally. Water sealers are easy to apply with an ordinary garden sprayer and can be "refreshed" with periodic applications. (If you see a dark stain on your deck after it rains, it's time for another coat.)

Cleaning a Deck

One of the simplest ways to keep a deck in pristine condition is to clean it regularly. I recommend that you follow the sequence *shown here* at a minimum of twice a year—once in the early spring and once in late fall. Cleaning a deck like this is analogous to flossing your teeth: You've got to get between deck boards, railings, and balusters to remove debris that can cause rot and decay, just as food trapped between teeth can cause tooth decay and cavities.

This sequence is simple and effective. The entire job, including optional pressure-washing (which I highly recommend), will take less than a few hours. It's time well spent to keep your deck structurally sound and looking new. Right after you've cleaned your deck, I also recommend that you give it a thorough visual inspection. Look for popped deck board nails or screws and any loose deck boards, railing, or balusters, and tighten or replace them as necessary.

1 **Sweep the deck** The first step in cleaning a deck is to sweep it well to remove any loose debris. A stiff-bristle "garage"-style broom works best. Pay particular attention to deck areas where parts butt up against each other. These will collect debris and are some of the areas most susceptible to rot and decay. That's because the debris traps water, which promotes the growth of mold, mildew, and fungus. This is very common on decks where the balusters run all the way to the deck boards, such as the one *shown here.*

2 **Mask off house and shrubs** Since most of the deck cleaning chemicals you'll be likely to use contain some form of acid (*see page 111*), the next step is to mask off the house to prevent the acid from discoloring the exterior of the house. You'll also want to protect any nearby plants and shrubs with drop cloths or plastic to prevent damage; *see the photo at right.* The same applies to your railing if you're not cleaning it; any sprayover or droplets can discolor an existing finish.

3 **Pressure-wash** When it comes to cleaning decks that are heavily stained or have a lot of caked-on dirt and grime, I like to pressure-wash the deck before applying a chemical cleaner (*see the photo at left*). This helps loosen stubborn dirt and allows you to blow debris out of corners and crevices. (If you don't own a pressure washer, you can pick one up for a day at most rental centers.) The best method is to start in the center of the deck and work your way out toward both ends.

4 **Spray on cleaner** Now you're ready to apply the cleaner or brightener. In most cases, the easiest way to apply it is with an ordinary pump garden sprayer (*see the photo at left*). Read and follow the manufacturer's directions—some want you to apply the chemical to a dry deck surface, while others want it wet. Also, some do not recommend using a garden sprayer and instead instruct you to apply it with a brush or roller. In any case, take care to apply it only where you want to clean and lighten the wood.

5 **Scrub with broom** After you've waited the specified time, you can rinse off the deck. But before you do this, inspect the deck for areas of discoloration. Although most chemicals say you don't need to scrub, you're sure to find spots or stains that would benefit from a little elbow grease. Most home centers sell brooms especially intended for cleaning decks; these typically have a short head and long, stiff bristles. Note that really stubborn stains may require several applications of cleaner followed by brisk scrubbing.

Finishing a Deck

Next to keeping your deck clean (*see pages 112–113*), keeping the finish on your deck in good order is the best way to increase the lifespan of your deck and keep it looking good. How often you need to reapply a finish to your deck will depend on its finish and on the local weather conditions. Decks exposed to extreme climates (such as the cold winters of Minnesota or the hot summers of Arizona) require more attention than a deck in a temperate region.

Likewise, the type of finish you use will affect the frequency of maintenance. Transparent water sealants often need to be refreshed every year, whereas solid-color stains may need attention less frequently. Note that although most composite decking doesn't require a finish, many of them will accept one—just realize that once you apply one, the finish will need regular attention.

1 **Sweep** The first thing you'll read on the directions of any can of deck finish is that the deck must be clean and free from dirt. If your deck is in fairly good shape, you may be able to get by with just a thorough sweeping (*see the photo at right*). If the deck is stained and dirty, you'll need to do a more complete cleaning, which may or may not include pressure-washing and use of a chemical cleaner; *see pages 112–113 for more on this*. Note that most finishes require a surface that's totally dry.

2 **Mask as needed** Depending on how you'll be applying the deck finish, you may want to mask off sensitive areas of the deck (like the door and the electrical outlet *shown here*). It is also wise to protect nearby plants and shrubs with drop cloths or plastic. This is particularly important when spraying on a finish using a garden sprayer or air-powered paint sprayer. If nothing else, you'll probably want to mask off the railing system since its vertical surfaces tend to need less refinishing work than the horizontal deck boards.

3 **Apply first coat** Now you're ready to apply the finish. Follow the manufacturer's directions for the number of coats and application. Some finishes are best applied with a garden sprayer. The manufacturer of the semitransparent deck stain *shown here* recommended applying the stain with a short-nap roller to get a more even coat. This way, when the inevitable puddling occurs, you can spread the finish out to prevent darker staining in these areas.

4 **Apply extra coat on edges** Although it's easy to concentrate on the flat horizontal surfaces of a deck, don't forget to protect the end of deck boards by brushing on a couple of coats of finish (*see the photo at left*). Sealing the ends of the boards is one of the best ways to prevent the board from soaking up moisture, which can cause it to split, cup, and twist. I like to wipe on several coats, allowing the finish to soak up into the ends between applications.

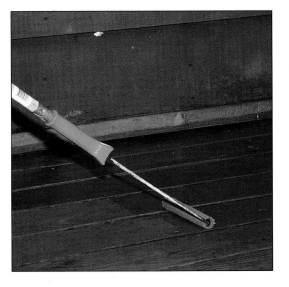

5 **Apply second coat** Whether or not you'll need to apply a second coat of finish will really depend on the type of finish and the level of protection you're after. Follow the manufacturer's directions to the letter here because the old adage "more is better" does not always apply. Many of these finishes are formulated for one-coat coverage, and laying down another coat may actually harm your deck—this is especially true with finishes designed to allow your deck boards to "breathe" as they react to changes in humidity.

Repairing Deck Boards

1 **Tighten loose boards** A loose or twisted deck board is one of the most common problems encountered with a wood deck. For a loose board, try driving in a screw or two at an angle, *as shown in the photo at right.* If you drive them in at opposing angles, the screws will lock the board to the joist. Make sure to use galvanized or stainless steel screws. To minimize the visual impact of the screw, use a trim-head screw. I don't recommend using nails at all here since they just don't have the holding power of a screw.

2 **Remove damaged board** If you find a board or boards that are beyond repair, you'll need to replace them. If the board is short, simply pry it up with a pry bar or crowbar (see *the photo at right*). If the damage is limited to one end of a long board, cut through the board directly over and centered above a joist as near as possible to the damage. A reciprocating saw that's fitted with a demolition blade is the best tool for this job. Then pry out the damaged section.

3 **Install new board** After you've removed the damage, the next step is to measure, mark, and cut a replacement board to length. Position the replacement deck board so there's an equal gap on each side, and then attach it to the underlying joists with galvanized or stainless steel screws. Don't forget to drill pilot holes near the ends of the replacement board to prevent splitting when the screws are driven in.

Replacing a Baluster

1 **Remove old baluster** How difficult or easy it is to replace a damaged baluster will depend on your railing system. On systems like the one *shown here,* where the baluster attaches to the railing and the fascia covering the rim joists, replacement is easy. If the baluster is screwed in place, back out the screws to remove it; otherwise pull it off by hand or with a crowbar. For systems where the balusters attach to top and bottom rails, you'll need to remove the fasteners in order to slide out the baluster.

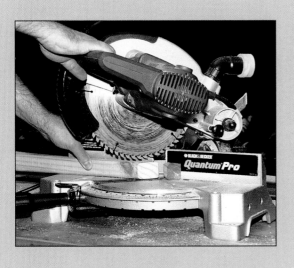

2 **Cut new baluster to fit** Carefully measure the length of an existing baluster (or the damaged one, if it's in one piece), and transfer this measurement to a replacement baluster. Cut the replacement baluster to length and check the fit to make sure it will slip into place. Note: If you can't find a replacement baluster at the local home center or lumberyard, check the yellow pages for fence companies in your area. Many of them stock a wide variety of balusters and porch spindles.

3 **Install replacement** Before you install the new baluster, it's a good idea to brush a coat or two of preservative onto the top and bottom of the baluster to help protect it from moisture damage. Next, drill pilot holes in the baluster for the fasteners you'll be using to attach it. This extra step will help prevent splitting as the screws are driven in. Now you can position the baluster, centered between its neighbors, and attach it with galvanized or stainless steel screws.

Repairing a Rail Post

1 **Remove old post** Rail posts, particularly those that are notched at the bottom to fit over the fascia (like the one *shown here*), have a tendency to split near the notch. When this occurs, it's a fairly straightforward task to replace it. To start, remove the old post by first detaching any connecting parts such as a deck cap and any rails. If these are screwed in place, back out the screws. Nailed-in pieces can be banged apart with a sledgehammer and a scrap of wood to protect the part. Then unscrew the post bolts and set the post aside.

2 **Make replacement post** If your old post is in one piece, use it as a template to make a replacement. Carefully measure its length and the notch (if applicable), and transfer these measurements to the replacement post. Cut the post to length and cut out the notch with a hand-saw or reciprocating saw. Then mark and drill countersunk shank holes for the lag bolts to match those on the original post. Finally, remove any splinters or rough edges with coarse sandpaper.

3 **Install new post** Now you can install the replacement post. As always, I recommend brushing a couple coats of preservative onto parts that will be concealed once the part is installed—in this case, the inside faces of the notch. Position the post and attach it to the deck with the original hardware. Then attach each of the connecting parts one at a time. If nails were used, I recommend removing these and replacing them with galvanized or stainless steel screws.

Replacing a Stair Tread

Replacing a damaged stair tread on a set of deck stairs is fairly uncomplicated. What can be complicated, however, is finding out what caused the damage. If the stair tread is warped, cupped, or twisted, it's probably simply reacting to the constant exposure to the elements. If the tread is left dirty and its finish has deteriorated, it's no wonder it warped. Sometimes this can be caused by the wood itself. In any case, remove the tread (*Step 1 below*) and replace it (*Step 2 below*). If, however, you notice that the tread is loose, angled, or wobbly, simply replacing it may not be enough; the actual damage may be in the stringer that it rests on. Remove the old tread, and check to make sure the stringer is fastened securely to both the deck and its footing. Then inspect the stringer itself for rot. Insert the point of a pocketknife into the edges of the stringer; if it slides in easily more than ¼", the stringer is rotten and should be replaced.

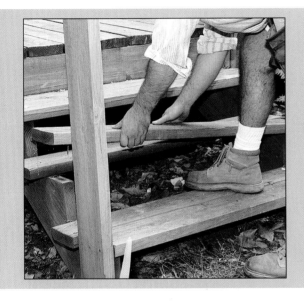

1 **Remove old tread** To remove a damaged tread, slip a pry bar under one end and lift up. Then grab the loose end and pull it up to remove it. For treads that are screwed in place, first back out the screws. If the tread is in one piece, set it aside so that you can use it as a template to measure and cut a replacement tread. Now is the time to inspect the stringer, regardless of the cause of the damage to the tread.

2 **Install new tread** Using the old tread as a template, measure, mark, and cut a replacement tread to length. Check the fit to make sure it matches the other treads before installing it. Also, make sure to drill pilot holes near the ends of the tread to prevent splitting when the screws are driven in. Center the tread on the stringer so the overhang (if any) is equal on both ends, and fasten it to the stringer with galvanized or stainless steel screws.

Repairing a Post

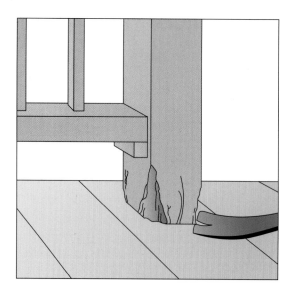

1 **Remove damage** Depending on the damage, it may not be necessary to replace an entire post. For posts where the damage is confined to a small area (particularly at the bottom of a post, *as shown here*), you can install a patch. Although it is possible to do this with the post in place, it's a whole lot easier if you first remove the post. To do this, remove any fasteners from connecting parts to separate them from the post, and then pry the post off the deck boards and remove it.

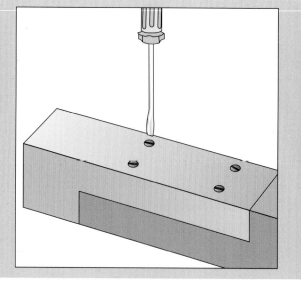

2 **Create half-lap joint** The best patch for the end of a post is to make an L-shaped piece like the one *shown in the drawing at right.* This joint is called a half-lap, as one-half of the joint is cut on each part. Measure, mark, and cut one-half of the joint on the post. Then cut the matching half on a piece of scrap post material. Attach the patch to the post with waterproof glue and galvanized or stainless steel screws.

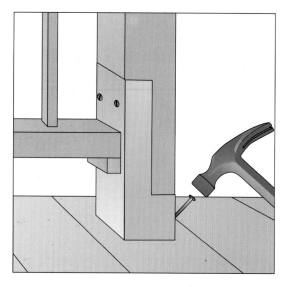

3 **Install new section** After the glue has dried, the patched post can be reinstalled. Before you do this, brush a coat or two of preservative onto the bottom of the post. Then set it in place and secure it to the deck with nails or screws. Next, reattach each connecting part one at a time. Note that you should always position the patch *as shown,* with the splice perpendicular to the edge of the deck. If you were to rotate it so the splice was parallel to the deck, it could easily crack when someone leans on the railing.

Repairing Skirting

1 **Remove old skirting** Since skirting or lattice that's used to conceal the foundation under a deck is often in contact with the ground, it has a tendency to rot and decay quickly. To replace damaged skirting, start by removing the old lattice. If it was screwed in place, back out the screws. If nailed, simply pry it off with a pry bar or crowbar (*see the photo at left*). Be careful not to damage the underlying frame that supports the lattice.

2 **Rebuild frame if necessary** In many cases where the skirting has rotted, the underlying support frame may be damaged. If this is the case, remove the old frame and install a new one. I usually use 2×2 pressure-treated lumber and attach the frame pieces to the foundation of the deck with galvanized screws (*see the photo at left*). I like to create an upside-down U by attaching 2×2 cleats to the sides as well. This creates a sturdy frame to support the lattice while minimizing contact with the ground.

3 **Attach new skirting** Once you've got a solid frame in place for the skirting, you can cut a piece to fit. If it will blend in with your other skirting, I recommend using plastic lattice. It can be cut with ordinary tools, requires no finish, and is virtually maintenance-free (*see the photo at left*). Measure, mark, and cut a piece to fit. Make sure there's at least an inch or two of clearance between the bottom of the lattice and the ground before you attach it to the frame with galvanized screws.

Replacing Porch Flooring

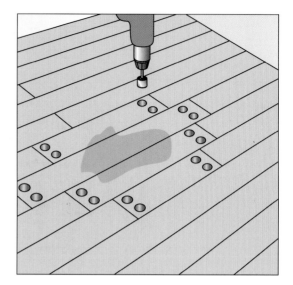

1 **Drill holes** To remove damaged porch flooring that's been installed with a staggered pattern, start by identifying the joints nearest the damage. Then, using a large spade bit, Forstner bit, or hole saw, drill a series of holes on the waste side of these joints, *as shown*. Mark the drilling depth with a strip of masking tape to match the thickness of the strip flooring so that you won't drill into the joist and weaken it.

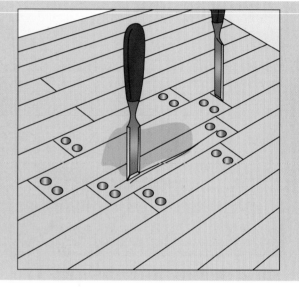

2 **Split strips with chisel** With a sharp chisel, break the nibs between the holes you drilled to free the ends of the strips. Then split the damaged strips in half lengthwise with a chisel and a mallet or hammer by driving the chisel into the middle of the strip, working your way down along its length. Don't be too aggressive here: It's easy to damage the adjacent strips, whose surface may crack or split under pressure.

3 **Add patch** Now you can remove the split pieces with a pry bar. Insert the end into a crack in the middle of a board and pry. If necessary, slip a small block of wood under the pry bar for added leverage and to protect adjacent strips. Then trim the edges of the cut area so it's square. Cut a patch to fit and install it with nails (*see the drawing at right*). Note: You'll need to insert the outermost strips first and then cut the lip off the bottom edge of the groove in the final strip in order to install it.

Repairing a Porch Column

Just like any other part of a porch, the columns that support the roof are susceptible to rot and decay. This most often occurs near the base of the column, where it attaches to the flooring, and usually results from lack of drainage. Because of the work involved in removing a porch column (raising the roof and then bracing it), it's a lot easier to repair the post in place. For posts where the damage is not structural, you can remove the damaged section (*see Step 1 below*) and rebuild it with an epoxy system manufactured by Abatron Inc. called WoodEpox (www.abatron.com). Like other epoxy systems, WoodEpox comes in two parts, both similar to putty. When mixed together in equal parts, it forms a pliable dough that can be easily sculpted and shaped. When hardened, it can be smoothed with regular tools and then painted to match the existing post.

1 Remove the damage To repair a damaged post, start by removing the rotted or decayed area. For small areas, use a chisel (*see the photo at left*). For larger areas, remove the damage with a handsaw. Take care to remove any punky areas as well. A large spade bit fitted in an electric drill works great for this. Remove any paint chips, dirt, or grime from the surrounding area to allow for a good bond of the epoxy dough.

2 Mix epoxy Mix the epoxy system by scooping out like-size lumps of resin paste and hardener paste and placing them on a clean, dry scrap of wood. The manufacturer suggests using a separate spoon for each to prevent contaminating the material left in the containers. After you've removed as much of each as you need, blend the two parts together. I find that a small putty knife works well for this. As long as you wear rubber gloves, you can even mix it by kneading it with your hands. In any case, make sure to mix it the full time recommended.

③ Apply the dough Once you've formed a nice, smooth dough that's uniform in color, you can apply it to the post. Here again, a small putty knife works great. Try and make the dough conform to the desired shape as well as possible, keeping in mind that you're better off having too much material than not enough. Also, take care to feather the dough near the edges to allow for a smooth transition between the damaged and undamaged areas.

④ Trim and shape After the dough has hardened the required time, you can trim and shape it as needed. A sharp chisel will quickly pare away unwanted areas; *see the photo at right.* A smooth mill file or wood rasp works well to quickly shape areas, too, and is particularly good for working on round columns.

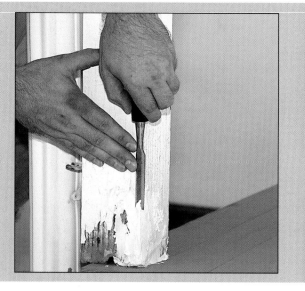

⑤ Sand the post Once you've achieved the desired shape, you can smooth the post with sandpaper, starting with coarse and working up to medium. Use an open-coat-type sandpaper, as this tends to clog less than other types. Pay particular attention to the transition between the epoxy dough and the undamaged area, to make sure it's smooth. Brush on a coat of primer and paint the damaged area to match the rest of the post.

Repairing a Brick Pier

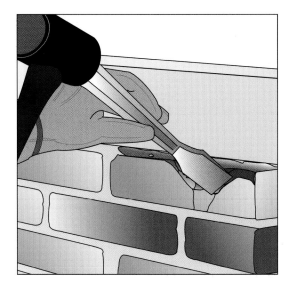

1 **Chisel out damage** Since the piers on a porch transfer the load of the porch to the footings, it's important that they be properly maintained. If you notice that one or more of the pier bricks are damaged, replace them immediately. Wearing leather gloves and eye protection, use a cold chisel and a sledgehammer to chip out the mortar and remove the damaged brick by prying it out. If this doesn't work, attack the brick itself and break it up into smaller pieces that can be levered out (*see the drawing at left*).

2 **Mix and apply new mortar** After you've removed the damaged brick and have cleaned out all the old mortar, wipe the cavity with a damp cloth. Mix enough mortar or concrete patching compound and then, using a trowel, apply a 1"-thick layer of mortar to the walls of the cavity and then a light coat to the brick itself (*see the drawing at left*).

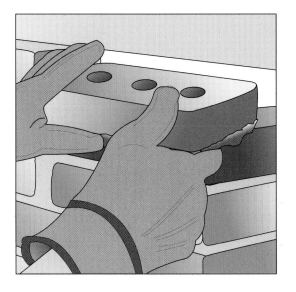

3 **Insert replacement brick** Slide the replacement brick into the cavity and push it in until its face is flush with the other bricks, tapping it in place with the end of the trowel as necessary (*see the drawing at left*). Use the trowel to fill in any gaps in the joints and then scrape off the excess. Smooth the joints with a gloved finger or a scrap of dowel.

Glossary

Above-ground – a grade of treated lumber intended for low to moderate decay hazards, where the wood will not be in contact with the ground.

Air nailer – any air-powered tool that shoots fasteners into a workpiece. When activated, compressed air forces a piston with an attached driver blade to drive the next fastener.

Attached deck – a deck that has one or more sides supported by a ledger and attached to a house.

Backfill – earth, sand, or gravel used to fill an excavated area, typically around a footing or pier.

Balusters – the vertical members of deck or porch railing that divide up the space between the posts.

Batter board – a horizontal board held in the ground via a pair of stakes, used to stretch a mason's line to locate footings.

Beam – a structural member that transfers joist loads to the posts.

Blocking – 2-by material installed between joists to provide rigidity to the foundation.

Bracing – 2-by members designed to reduce the tendency of a deck or porch to rack.

Cantilever – a construction method where a frame extends out past the foundation; also can refer to the overhang itself.

Cap rail – a railing member that is laid flat horizontally across the tops of posts.

Column – structural members designed to transfer the roof load to the porch foundation.

Composite decking – any of a number of hybrid deck board products manufactured by combining sawdust or wood chips with plastic.

Deck board – the floor board of a deck.

Deck cleaner – a chemical that's used to strip away dirt and grime from deck boards; may include a mild acid (usually oxalic acid) to "brighten" or bleach the surface of the deck.

Drip edge - a bent metal strip that fits over the edge of the ledger to direct rain away from the ledger and underlying walls.

Elevated deck – a deck that requires footings and posts to raise it to the desired level; typically used to make the deck match the height of the interior floors.

Elevation – a side view of a structure that shows vertical dimensions and relationships; an elevation section shows a vertical slice of a structure.

Face-nail – to drive a nail through one piece and into another with the nail at a right angle to the surface.

Fascia – nonstructural decorative trim installed around the perimeter of a deck or porch to cover the joists.

Flooring – typically 1×4 tongue-and-groove boards installed across the joists, perpendiclar to the house.

Footing – a unit (usually concrete) used to support a post to transfer the deck or porch load to the ground.

Framing connectors – a wide range of metal fasteners used to connect wood parts; a joist hanger is an example of a framing connector.

Freestanding deck – a self-supporting deck that's not attached to a house or other structure.

Frost line – the maximum depth at which freezing can occur; varies depending on location.

Galvanized fastener – any fastener coated with zinc to retard corrosion; the most effective method of galvanizing is a process called hot-dipping, where the individual fasteners are dipped in molten zinc.

Ground-contact – a grade of treated lumber intended for high-decay hazards, as when in contact with the ground.

Handrail – horizontal members installed between columns or newel posts.

Joist – a structural wood member that supports deck or flooring boards and spans the frame.

Knee rails – rails installed 3' above the perimeter of the porch; often used to support screening.

Lattice – wood or plastic strips formed into a grid used for screens and skirting.

Ledger – a structural member that attaches to the house and supports one end of the joists.

Line level – a small bubble level that hangs from a mason's line; typically used to level a post or beam with respect to a ledger.

Multilevel deck – a deck that has discrete areas at different levels; frequently used to conform to sloping terrain.

Newel post – a vertical member that supports a handrail where there is no column.

Overhang – the portion of a deck or porch that extends beyond the posts or beams; often called a cantilever.

Pier – a brick or concrete unit that supports a column, header, or beam.

Plan view – a view of a structure shown from above—a bird's-eye view. A plan view of a deck or porch shows the foundation framing or the decking.

Post – a structural member that supports a beam and transfers the deck or porch load to the footing.

Post anchor – a special metal fastener used to anchor a post to a footing, most often a J-bolt.

Post-hole digger – a special tool used to dig holes for footings; often referred to as a clamshell digger.

Power auger – a portable power tool designed to bore large-diameter holes in the ground for footings; available at most rental centers.

Preservative – a chemical used to protect wood from decay.

Pressure-treated lumber – lumber, typically Southern yellow pine, that is impregnated with a preservative (usually chromated copper arsenate) to repel insects and retard rot.

Radius-edge decking (RED) – lumber produced for decking: 1" thick and 5½" wide with rounded edges.

Railing – a portion of a deck or porch designed to enclose it; typically consists of a rail post, cap rail, and balusters.

Ring-shank nails – nails that are manufactured with rings along the shank to provide extra grip.

Rise – the vertical distance from one stair to another.

Riser – the vertical portion of a step or stairway, designed to support the treads.

Rough opening – an opening that's sized to accept a window or door; a horizontal framing member called a header is installed to assume the load of the wall studs that were removed; the header is supported by jack studs that are attached to full-length wall studs.

Run – the horizontal distance from one stair riser to another, or the depth of the step.

Screening – metal or fiberglass mesh installed around the perimeter of a porch to keep out insects.

Site plan – a map of the lot showing the land, landscaping, and other features.

Skirt – a screen installed below a deck or porch to hide the foundation and limit access.

Spindle – a type of baluster that's turned on a lathe to create a distinctive round profile.

Stringer – the diagonal section of steps that supports risers and treads.

Toenail – to drive a nail at an angle through one piece and into another.

Tread – the horizontal portion of stairway—the step.

Index